Smaller

HEALTHY

GROWING

EXTRAORDINARY MINISTRY

Barry Campbell

LifeWay Press
Nashville, Tennessee

ISBN 0-7673-9126-8

Dewey Decimal Classification: 254

Subject Heading: CHURCH ADMINISTRATION \ SMALLER CHURCHES

Printed in the United States of America.

Cover Photo: DR Productions/David Rogers

Pastor-Staff Leadership Department

LifeWay Christian Resources of

The Southern Baptist Convention

127 Ninth Avenue, North

Nashville, Tennessee 37234

DEDICATION

This book is dedicated to my precious wife, Marci. For most of her life she has been either the daughter or wife of a smaller church pastor. Her keen insight and gift of discernment have proven extremely valuable in the smaller membership churches where we have labored together. Her tireless work and abundant talents make her an ideal partner in smaller church ministries.

ACKNOWLEDGEMENTS

Not only has Judi Hayes served faithfully and well as editor of this book, but her help was also invaluable in researching and pulling together the stories of the Gardena-Torrance Southern Baptist Church in Los Angeles, California, and Hillside Baptist Church in Anchorage, Alaska. Ed Rowell also helped gather information on the Emmanuel Baptist Church in Carrolton, Michigan.

INTRODUCTION

Smaller membership churches are important in the kingdom of God. It has often been my privilege to lead training sessions for smaller membership church pastors. These precious kingdom leaders are sometimes surprised to learn how many other churches are similar in size to theirs. The vast majority of Baptist churches have fewer than one hundred in attendance on a typical Sunday morning. In fact most of them have a lot fewer. Smaller membership churches make up more than 60 percent of all our churches.

This book is written with two simple objectives. The first objective is to tell the stories of six healthy, smaller membership churches. The churches are from different parts of the country. Some are led by fully funded pastors; others, by bivocational pastors. Some of the churches are creative and contemporary in their approach, while others are traditional. They were chosen as a sample of some of the excellent ministry done in our smaller churches.

While the churches presented here are diverse in many ways, they also have some things in common. Each of these smaller churches has health that comes from a balanced approach to ministry. To show that balance I have used a similar format in telling about each of these churches. The church's stories are told in the framework of the five functions of the church. Each church is effective in evangelism, discipleship, fellowship, ministry, and worship. They may use different methods and approaches, but they fulfill each of theses functions, and they do so in a healthy manner.

The second objective of the book is to present some practical, useable ideas to help smaller membership churches fulfill these five functions in a healthy manner. To that end, part II of the book is a showcase of ideas organized around the five functions.

I am convinced that smaller membership churches can achieve balance, health, and growth. One effective way to get a handle on all we do is intentionally to plan to fulfill each of these five essential functions of the church. As churches do this, they will achieve balance and health.

CONTENTS

Chapter 1

THE 1-5-4 PRINCIPLE

In his book, *Kingdom Principles for Church Growth*, Gene Mims introduced us to the 1•5•4 principle. It's simple. The church has one Great Commission, five functions, and four results of carrying out those functions in a healthy manner.

I was a pastor for 18 years. Looking back on those 18 years, I'm convinced that my leadership of the church was just a little bit out of focus. During those 18 years my primary focus was church growth. I wanted to reach people for Christ, and I wanted my church to grow. It wasn't about numbers; it was about people, but the primary focus was church growth. The 1•5•4 Principle suggests, and I agree, that church growth is a result, not a function or a goal. When we focus on doing the five functions that every church ought to do and do those five functions in a healthy manner, church growth will result. Church growth will be a by-product of doing the things every church ought to do. Our focus can be church health instead of church growth, and church growth will become a naturally expected result of doing the things every church should do.

1 Great Commission

We know about the one Great Commission. That's our marching orders. In the Great Commission the Lord instructed us to go into all the world, make believers, and baptize them into local churches. We need to teach them all the things that Jesus has taught us.

5 Essential Functions

The next part of the 1•5•4 Principle suggests that the church has five functions—that is, five things every church ought to do. And when a church does those five things in a healthy manner, church growth will result. Every church ought to be involved in evangelism, discipleship, fellowship, ministry, and worship. These are not listed in order of priority. They are simply the things every church should do.

4 Expected Results

The 1•5•4 Principle also reminds us that four results will take place when a church does the five functions in a healthy manner.

Numerical growth.—Almost every smaller membership church ought to be growing numerically. If you are doing evangelism in a healthy manner, you are reaching people for Christ. If you are doing discipleship in a healthy manner, you are teaching those people in Bible study and in other discipleship ministries. If you are doing ministry and fellowship in a healthy manner, then you are assimilating and keeping those people; and if you are doing worship in a healthy manner, you are leading them into an encounter with God Himself. This should produce numerical growth in almost every situation.

Some churches may be in communities where the population is decreasing so rapidly that even though the church is doing the five functions in a healthy manner numerical growth will not be registered at the end of the year. Perhaps due to a plant closing or some other demographic phenomenon, the church is decreasing in size—even though the church is fulfilling the five functions in a healthy manner. Occasionally I've seen a situation where a pastor is doing the five functions in a healthy manner, but his church is so unhealthy, so divided, so wounded, that numerical growth cannot and will not take place. Except for these kinds of rare exceptions, almost every smaller membership church should be increasing in size. Numerical growth is biblical, and we ought to be involved in growing our churches. But, remember church growth, numerical growth, is not the function or the goal; it is a result. When we do these five functions in a healthy manner, church growth will result.

Spiritual growth.—I used to think that spiritual growth couldn't be measured, but a few months ago I preached in a smaller membership church. I arrived on Sunday morning, preached in their Sunday morning service, and then I returned on Sunday night. The church had about 100 in attendance on Sunday morning, but more than 40 adults returned for a new *Experiencing God* class on Sunday night. If that smaller membership church has more than 40 people participating in an *Experiencing God* course, they can measure some spiritual growth in that church. Take seriously the expectation that your people will grow spiritually, that they will become stronger and more mature as disciples. When you do the five functions in a healthy manner, spiritual growth will take place.

Missions advance.—Every church should be involved in missions, and it's important for every church to expect this result. If you are doing missions, you are going to be doing one of those five functions. You are winning people or teaching people or leading people in worship, or ministering to people, or fellowshipping with people. As you do those things, the people's participation in missions will grow. In fact, it stands to reason that missions involvement will increase as God's people participate in those missions opportunities.

Increase in ministry.—Your people will be involved in ministry. A healthy church, a balanced church is a church where the people are doing ministry, and this is multiplied as lots of people in the church get involved in ministry.

Notice something about this 1•5•4 Principle. A church that does the five functions in a healthy manner will achieve both balance and focus. The church will be balanced because it will intentionally approach each of the five functions. What are we going to do this year about evangelism? What will we do to carry out the discipleship function? How will we enhance our worship experience this year? How will we be sure we are ministering and fellowshipping in a healthy manner? The church that is balanced in carrying out the five functions will be a healthy church. Not only does the church achieve balance, but it also achieves focus because the church zeros its attention in on each one of those five functions individually and intentionally as it accomplishes each of the five functions. A church has balance because it does each of the five functions. It has focus because it looks intentionally at each of the five functions, and a church can be a healthy church by achieving the balance and focus of carrying out those five functions in the church.

Part 1

THE
CHURCHES

ANCHORAGE, ALASKA

CARLETON, MICHIGAN

LOS ANGELES, CALIFORNIA

PICAYUNE, MISSISSIPPI

LYNNVILLE, TENNESSEE

CALIENTE, NEVADA

Chapter 2

HILLSIDE BAPTIST CHURCH

Matthew and Stephanie Friese could serve anywhere. This young, dynamic, seminary-trained couple understand the balance needed to grow a church. They have the needed skills. They work hard and love the Lord. They would be an asset to any church. God called them to serve near home, and they are growing a church in Anchorage, Alaska. High-school friends and family are less than a hundred miles away.

The email address for Hillside Baptist Church in Anchorage, Alaska, begins *HBCGodatwork*, and He is! Pastor Matt is leading the small congregation (It won't be small for long!) to exciting growth and ministry.

Hillside began in 1970. During the early 1990s, Mississippi Baptists partnered with the church to help provide their current facility—a neat and attractive two-story facility on the edge of Anchorage, near the Alaska Baptist State Convention building. The lower level provides space for education and fellowship. The upper floor provides education space and the auditorium. Additional education space is provided in three small buildings behind the main facility. Those buildings, too, are attractive, matching the main building in color and style.

The church's mission statement is important to the congregation. It appears frequently in print and resides permanently above the entrance to the auditorium: "To bring people into God's family through the saving knowledge of eternal life in Christ Jesus, develop them to Christlike maturity, and equip them for their ministry in the church and harvest field in order to magnify God."

Matt and Stephanie came to Hillside in 1994. Both are native Alaskans; both studied at Southwestern Baptist Theological Seminary. Matt served churches while in seminary, but Hillside is his first church since completing his degree. He's an energetic 28-year-old who is making a difference in Anchorage as both a resident and a minister.

Evangelism

Matt quickly points out that he alone is not responsible for the growth at Hillside. Of course, he always credits God first. Then he acknowledges the work of Hillside's laypeople.

One of the reasons for the growth Hillside has seen is the emphasis on weekly outreach and evangelism. He began with two teams, then four. This fall Matt anticipates having seven teams to go out each week.

When teams do not have enough prospects or absentees to visit, Matt is working on a plan where they will go into every member's home and work with members to help each member write a personal testimony. Matt wants to keep these on file so that he knows for certain the relationship all of his members have with Jesus Christ. He believes that he can provide more effective pastoral ministry when he does not simply assume he knows a member's relationship to Christ.

Discipleship

Sunday School has grown during the past three years from an average attendance of 40 to 120. In addition to Sunday School, the church has begun many more opportunities for discipleship.

The church has had a strong prayer ministry on Wednesday nights. They are now adding opportunities for additional midweek studies. Recently all the adults studied *The Baptist Faith and Message*. Most of Hillside's members did not grow up in Christian homes. Learning Baptist distinctives has become an important part of their discipleship.

The church has also used a number of the LifeWay resources such as *Making Peace with Your Past*. These have benefitted the congregation, but they have also ministered to persons in the community.

Sunday School teachers have additional opportunities for study. They are asked to sign a covenant when they become teachers. The responsibility to teach others is taken seriously. Teachers are expected to be faithful, to prepare well, and to participate in training opportunities. Part of that training includes becoming alert and prepared for teachable moments, following Jesus' example, to teach as they intersect with members in their daily lives.

Fellowship

Building relationships and providing times for fellowship become even more significant in a state where most citizens are thousands of miles away from families. In this unique situation the church has decided to provide special times for the entire church to be together during holidays.

Over the July 4 weekend the church secures an entire campground at nearby Seward, a beautiful town on the coast of the Kenai peninsula. The town itself has a big celebration each year, including a run up Marathon Mountain, rising more than 3,200 feet behind the town.

At Thanksgiving members gather at Alaska Baptist Convention's youth camp for a congregational feast. Other relationship-building times include the church's active men's and women's ministries. And Sunday School classes include a fellowship event at least every 6–13 weeks.

Ministry

Matt has led the congregation in having a comprehensive approach to ministry from evangelism and discipleship to community responsibility. The church provides traditional ministries such as a food pantry and rental and utility assistance. But the church also adopted a section of a road to keep clean. Seeing Hillside Baptist Church on that road sign is a reminder to the community that kingdom citizens can also be good citizens of Anchorage.

Matt and Stephanie have also had opportunities to counsel individual members of the church and community. Stephanie's experience as a marriage and family counselor has allowed the church to expand ministry to individuals and groups.

Worship

Matt describes the worship services as a blend of traditional and contemporary. The congregation seems to enjoy both familiar hymns and praise choruses.

Matt occasionally preaches topical sermons and occasionally offers more creative messages, such as dramatic monologues, but most of the time his messages are expository. He says he really enjoys preaching God's Word, and expository messages allow him to focus on biblical truth. He plans intentionally to make the Bible passages relevant to his young congregation. It is so important, in fact, that the church's yellow pages ad includes the phrase, "Experience the Relevancy of God."

Matt has added opportunities for children and youth to worship. Youth enjoy their JAM Sessions (Jesus and Me). The youth group has grown so much that the church has called a part-time youth minister.

The children's special time with Pastor Matt every Sunday is called Pastor's Pals, a children's sermon, after which they leave for children's worship. Children have this opportunity every Sunday during both morning worship services.

Though Matt is reluctant to talk about numbers, they are impressive. When he arrived at the church, the congregation had been without a pastor for two years. Average worship attendance was 50–60. Now, including both the 8:30 and the 11:00 worship services, attendance in worship averages about 160–175. Matt is baptizing 25–30 each year, but he adds that less than 10 percent of the population of Anchorage is a member of any church. Many more need to hear the good news of Jesus Christ.

Results

Membership and attendance are not the only numbers increasing. Financial giving has also continued to escalate. During the past three years the church budget has grown from $60,000 to $190,000. The church paid off its $188,000 debt on the building in one year.

The numbers are the first evidence of growth at Hillside, but the growth does not end there. Pastor Matt says he sees many ways in which members have matured in discipleship. He says their increasing spiritual depth is evidenced in their faithfulness and in their ability to relate better to one another. Conflicts resulting from growth, which once would have been divisive, now are handled calmly; and members move on to the next growth challenge and opportunity.

New ministries are also beginning. The Family to Family plan is rooted in deacon ministry. Each deacon and his wife work with several families; and each of those families, in turn, minister to several families. The goal is for deacons to train and equip more couples for servant leadership.

With the building debt paid off and the budget increased, Hillside has also increased its mission giving, providing up to $30,000 each year for missions—almost one sixth (15.79%) of its annual budget. And the church doesn't stop its interest in missions with financial gifts.

Last year the church worked with more than one hundred people who came from Georgia to help Hillside. Together they visited every home in the two square miles around the church, approximately seven thousand homes. This year the church is working with the association in the Mission Anchorage Good News campaign.

This summer the church is hosting 40 volunteers from Georgia. While they will help Hillside, the host church has planned ways for volunteers to help smaller churches with Vacation Bible School and other projects.

The church supports missions near and far. They work in and support mission churches in remote portions of Alaska, and last year a team from the church traveled to Guatemala. Planning has already begun for a mission trip to Kenya in 1999.

The church also works in community projects. It assists in youth centers and senior adult shelters. The church has housed a Boy Scout troop, hosted CPR training, and provided space for voter registration.

Perhaps the most interesting new ministry—at least to Southern Baptists in the lower 48, is its roadkill ministry. Every year several hundred moose are killed on the highways. Hillside, like some other community agencies, is planning to provide ways to butcher the meat for distribution to needy families. The bruised meat is discarded, and the meat is tested and processed, so those receiving it are assured of its usefulness.

Hillside more than lives up to its yellow pages ad. God is at work at Hillside, and in every way they make sure Anchorage knows that God is as relevant today as ever.

Chapter 3

EMMANUEL BAPTIST CHURCH

The church property was alive with activity. People were attentively watching a two-minute drama performed from a makeshift stage on the back of a flatbed truck. Children were playing in a moonwalk. Others were enjoying face painting or the clown ministry. Everyone was enjoying plenty of free food. Throughout the crowd church members were meeting people from the community. Church members could be overheard saying: "We're glad you came. Did you get your free gift?" The gift was a marked New Testament with a little information about the church. Many were able to share the gospel as they presented the marked New Testaments.

Pastor David Jones, of Emmanuel Baptist Church in Carleton, Michigan, was amazed at the results of this block party. The church is located right in town, at a place where many from the community would pass by. Pastor Jones reports that the block party reached people who would never have attended church. But the block party is not the only creative ministry happening at Emmanuel.

In 1991, when David Jones came to be pastor of Emmanuel, attendance was 15–20 people on a good Sunday. The church is located in Carleton, Michigan, between Detroit, Michigan, and Toledo, Ohio. It's a small town, actually a bedroom community for Detroit. Most of the people work in one of the automobile manufacturing businesses. Homes are expensive to purchase as people move out of Detroit to the small-town atmosphere of Carleton.

Two financial and social extremes exist in the community. Some have low-paying jobs, while others have high-paying blue collar or engineering jobs. The diversity of the people presents situations where strongly differing opinions emerge. For example, labor and management issues come up from time to time. Pastor Jones reports that "the spirit of Christ keeps them in a bond." What these people have in common is more significant than anything that might divide them.

Even though the church is growing, and a great spirit is evident at Emmanuel, everything has not always been easy for David Jones and his family. Leading a smaller church to grow is hard work and can be discouraging. Brother Jones knows what it's like to plan a worship service but have no one available to provide accompaniment for the music. He has experienced the pain of working and praying through church conflict. Like many smaller church pastors, Jones has known the discouragement that comes from being the target of malicious statements meant to hurt him.

During those difficult days, Pastor Jones reminded himself that his motivation for ministry was his "love for the Lord" and nothing else. His focus was and is on his relationship to the Lord, and from that relationship comes the ministry. Because of a focus on his relationship to the Lord, Pastor Jones has found the strength to stay through those discouraging times. In fact, Jones is convinced that people trust him more because they have seen him stay during hard times. They know he won't run at the first sign of hardship. David Jones has earned the right to lead.

Emmanuel is organized for effectiveness. Pastor Jones, who has an undergraduate degree in business administration, calls his volunteer key leaders a "leadership team." Jones admits that it is actually a Church Council, but he prefers the term *leadership team*. He is convinced that members of a team are more likely to work to accomplish their goals. The leadership team has the freedom to "catch the vision and run with it." They are the ones in the trenches, actually doing the ministry. Pastor Jones sees his role as providing an overall vision for the church, keeping everyone connected in the different ministries, and keeping everyone moving in the same direction.

The future is bright for Pastor David Jones and Emmanuel Baptist Church. Since 1991, attendance has grown from 20 to more than 160. The congregation has purchased 15 acres about half a mile from their present location and will soon begin work on a new building. The congregation is excited about what God has done, but they are even more excited about what God will do. Here are some specific examples of how Emmanuel carries out the functions of the church.

Evangelism

Fishing derby.—When the men of Emmanuel told Pastor Jones they wanted to have a fishing derby, he thought the fishermen in the church were just looking for an excuse to go fishing. But he changed his mind when, last year, a half dozen people accepted Christ as a result of the fishing derby. It's a family event. Almost any lake or pond with fish makes a good location. A few small prizes are given, and relationships are developed.

Christmas dinner.—The biggest event of the year at Emmanuel is the Christmas dinner. The church rents a hall somewhere away from the church building. The meal is catered, and the cost is covered by those attending. Special speakers and music are chosen to communicate well with the unchurched community.

Vacation Bible School.—VBS is an effective form of event evangelism at Emmanuel. As the children move through several stations of learning activities, special attention is given the parents. Volunteers join the parents as they wait to pick up their children. Relationships are built at every opportunity.

Block party.—Pastor David Jones first began to consider the idea of a block party when he attended a conference on the subject. In fact, the conferees actually participated in a block party. Some of the details were mentioned above, and here are a few more.

Emmanuel Baptist Church is located near five mobile home parks. In fact, every time a resident leaves one of the parks, they have to face the church property. The leadership team decided to use the church's location to try to reach some of these people with the gospel. The block party was located on the church property.

After almost a year of planning, drama, free food, clowns, face painting, and lots of other activities were used to make the party fun and inviting for the community. Church members in casual dress distributed free New Testaments and told people about Jesus and His church.

Personal testimonies.—Pastor Jones enlists two or three people to give their personal testimonies at a Sunday evening service. Because they are enlisted in advance, those sharing testimonies can tell their story effectively.

Discipleship

Sunday School.—Sunday School is at the heart of the discipleship function at Emmanuel Baptist Church. The children's Sunday School is different from most. Children move through several stations where teachers lead 15-minute sessions. The teachers teach the same thing several times and adapt the lesson for the age group present.

Monthly Sunday School worker training meetings are an important part of the discipleship strategy. Pastor Jones uses this time to train his workers and plan the work of the Sunday School. He teaches them that Sunday School is the ministry unit of the church. He also says that Sunday School groups keep relationships flowing. Through the small groups of Sunday School, members can know the needs of members and prospects and organize themselves to meet those needs. Sunday School is the outreach evangelism component of the church.

Sunday School is so significant in fulfilling all the functions of the church that Sunday School workers are asked to sign a commitment that they will serve faithfully as members of the Sunday School leadership team. Sunday School is the key method of assimilation in the church. Pastor Jones emphasizes the importance of assimilating prospects and new members through the Sunday School when he says, "When you just bring them into the worship service, they're most likely going to get lost." In the Sunday School, "you already have established relationships, and that's how we've been able to keep tabs on people."

Sunday Night Semesters.—On Sunday nights Emmanuel offers

small-group studies such as *Experiencing God, Search for Significance,* or structured Bible studies.

Fellowship

Fellowship is more than picnics and other opportunities for food and fun. These activities do, however, play an important part in a complete, healthy approach to fellowship in the church. Here are a few other ways to approach the fellowship function.

Fellowship can grow through working together. While doing ministry, fellowship is built. Pastor Jones tells of a Saturday morning when the men of the church gathered to paint the home of a senior citizen. During the six hours of work, the men began to connect with one another in new ways. They felt good about doing something for the Lord, and they also got to know one another.

Fellowship can grow through commitment to the body of Christ. Pastor Jones says: "They can be members of the church but not part of the fellowship. Fellowship is where they really connect to the body and become part of the body."

Fellowship can grow through conflict. This surprising insight came as Pastor Jones realized that conflict can do one of two things. it can destroy a body, or it can strengthen the body. Fellowship occurs as people walk through conflict together. As a congregation is forced by conflict to keep the focus on Jesus and maintain unity, fellowship is strengthened.

Ministry

The five functions of the church are not always separate and distinct form one another. A healthy church will find that one function is fulfilled in the pursuit of another. Doing ministry, for example, is a wonderful and effective way to build fellowship. The same ministry will include discipleship and even evangelism. So when the people of Emmanuel gather to do ministry projects, many functions are addressed.

From repairing leaky roofs to installing a hot water heater, the people of Emmanuel are involved in ministry. They also enjoy participation in a food closet ministry, and they join other churches in their association in a ministry to migrant farm workers in the community.

Worship

The people of Emmanuel enjoy creative, blended worship. On Sunday morning musical accompaniment is provided by a piano. On Sunday and Wednesday nights a guitar is used. They are moving in the direction of adding more instruments in the future. Drama is incorporated three or four times a month.

Pastor Jones has preached on worship and taught his people that "worship is not a spectator sport." As a result, the people of Emmanuel don't want to observe worship. They want to participate. A shallow experience is inadequate; they want to be involved. A children's sermon and personal testimonies are used to involve people. The services are designed to be as interactive as possible.

The people of Emmanuel look forward to the day when they can worship in their new multipurpose building. They own 15 acres and are planning the building that will be their new home. They realize that the effectiveness of a church is not determined by its building. They have, after all, been healthy and effective since 1991 in their present facility. But they look forward to occupying their new facility and using it as a tool to be even more effective in fulfilling the Great Commission in their community.

Chapter 4

GARDENA-TORRANCE SOUTHERN BAPTIST CHURCH

Pastor Ted Knapp has served Gardena-Torrance Southern Baptist Church for 22 years. For the past 9 years he has served as pastor.

Gardena-Torrance is located in a multiracial, multiethnic community. The congregation includes Anglos, Hawaiians, and African-Americans. For more than 30 years the church has also shared its space with a Japanese congregation, an independent mission of Gardena-Torrance.

The church is surrounded by single-family homes and small apartment complexes. For years the church occupied a two-story building and adjacent housing, which they used as educational space. The auditorium was located on the first floor of the main building, with additional educational space on the second level. Through the years the property fell behind in meeting California's strict codes for public buildings. Repeatedly the church was warned to update its facility, but funds were scarce. They continued to focus on people and ministry needs rather than buildings.

Then the unthinkable happened. About the time Ted became pastor, the city condemned the facility. The church-owned homes and the second story of the main building were closed. Suddenly the church faced a crisis decision. They could shut the doors of the church, merge with another church, or enter a challenging building project. The congregation chose to build. While Sunday School classes met in every corner from closets to the baptistry, Ted began to think about the ideal facility for this particular church in this particular place. He dreamed of providing space to meet the needs of additional ethnic groups in the neighborhoods. This seemed to be the perfect opportunity to consider that venture.

Ted's engineering background and organizational skills came in handy. They designed a multiuse facility with a price tag of $450,000. Doing much of the work themselves, the facility ended up costing $150,000 more than projected. The church is still working to pay off the last $50,000. A major, unforeseen expense was an elevator—a unplanned luxury that California law required.

Sometimes during those building years, Ted worked all night long. While he worked, he dreamed of sharing the space—God's space—with other ethnic groups. He had a vision to share more than space. His vision included mutual respect and freedom among the congregations.

Just before the building was condemned, a Chinese church joined the the other two congregations. Los Angeles Crenshaw Baptist Church will soon celebrate its 35th anniversary. Members decided to relocate to an area with more Chinese-speaking residents. Currently this congregation is celebrating the arrival of a new pastor, Jonathan Chan.

Pastor Knapp believed there was room for one more congregation. Three years ago Peter Han, pastor of the Podowon Baptist Church, brought a prayer request to a pastors' meeting in Crescent Bay Association. His congregation needed a new home.

Ted took the request back to the three established congregations. Knowing that adding a Korean congregation would bring ancient enemies into one facility, he was unsure how everyone would react. The pastors agreed that if any congregation voted against sharing space with Podowon, the invitation would not be extended. All voted to welcome this new congregation. The Korean church quickly grew to become the largest congregation. Almost all the growth is conversion growth, and Pastor Han has already baptized 11 during the first half of 1998.

The church building always hums with activity. All the congregations worship on Sunday. With two auditoriums, the congregations plan their schedules so that two have Sunday School while the other two have worship services. With planning meetings, choir practice, fellowships, lunches, and other activities, one or more congregations have something scheduled on Sunday without a break from 8:00 a.m. until late afternoon.

Sunday is not the only busy day. The Koreans, for example, begin every day with a prayer meeting at 5:45 a.m., and they teach a Discipleship Training course four nights a week.

Calendaring is a key to the success of the shared space. After the annual calendar is planned, facilities' use is on a first-come basis. A master calendar is posted. If a room is not scheduled for use, any congregation can add an event at any time. No one else need give "permission."

The secret to their success begins long before the calendar is planned. Pastor Knapp decided that he did not want to share his space with anyone. He never believed it was his to share. He knew that the chances of his reaching these diverse language groups was much smaller than if they could worship in their own language. He praises God for each person who enters any one of the congregations—and thus enters God's kingdom.

With the twin concepts of mutual freedom and respect always shaping the decisions made, the pastors and congregations work together. Pastor Knapp says: "Respect and freedom must be the cornerstone. These concepts must be preached from the pulpit, taught, seen from leaders, stated and restated to the congregation. A visible and verbal respect and equality of all other cultures, languages, and races must be the norm."

The congregations share expenses on a somewhat equal basis. Because all feel ownership, they try to contribute—and share—whatever is needed. For example, when the new auditorium needed a piano and a sound system, the Korean community purchased it. Of course, the Chinese congregation uses it every week.

Each congregation has a Church Council. A joint council is responsible for the annual calendar and other mutual concerns. The pastor and two members from each congregation serve on the council. Responsibility for leading the council rotates among the pastors.

Their system for handling disputes is biblically based. When one pastor is made aware of a problem, he first checks to see if a member of his own congregation could be at fault. If he determines that is not the case and thinks it is the other congregation that primarily shares the space, he goes privately to that pastor only. Only when problems are mounting and cannot be solved privately are they taken to the joint council to resolve. This plan teaches mutual respect among all members. Pastor Knapp says, "Keep your focus on the ministry of reaching people for Christ Jesus, and the problems will always remain small and manageable."

Once a year the congregations worship together, then share a potluck meal that celebrates the cuisines of all the groups. They worship together in an Easter sunrise service (followed by a potluck breakfast). Sometimes congregations join for VBS.

Evangelism

The pastors visit in the community, meeting residents of their language-culture groups. Every first-time visitor receives a "sweet visit," usually an apple pie. Planned events include community surveys done with the assistance of summer missionaries.

VBS is always an outreach tool. Other outreach programs for children include Kids First, which uses TeamKid resources.

The evangelistic focus in the Chinese congregation is on breaking down barriers and developing relationships. The new pastor has asked church members to invite him to any gathering—family, business, social, or community—so that he can establish relationships and let everyone know of his concern and availability.

Almost every member of the Japanese congregation carries a special burden for reaching others. Many Japanese are in the United States as students or businessmen and women sent to learn the language and business culture. Both groups return to Japan after a few years. Most are Buddhist, and conversion is a slow process. In addition to witnessing, members of Gardena-Torrance feel strongly that they should live exemplary lifestyles so that their behavior is above reproach.

The Koreans say their most effective evangelistic strategy is prayer. They have a daily prayer meeting at 5:45 a.m. When members encounter friends with problems, they suggest they come to pray with them. They are not asked to come once to pray but to make a commitment to come for six to eight weeks. During the prayer services the pastor preaches through biblical highlights on a two-year schedule. If non-Christians begin to attend prayer meetings, the pastor has ample opportunity to present Christ and biblical truths to relate to their needs.

Discipleship

The Korean church offers discipleship courses using LifeWay resources, such as *Experiencing God*, four nights a week. New Christians have opportunity to grow quickly into leadership roles.

The Anglo congregation has monthly Christian Growth Training Workshops, weeknight cell group Bible studies, youth retreats, and training events. The pastor includes Discipleship Training as a part of council meetings. Church leaders to read and study leadership books.

A special discipleship plan the pastor has developed meets needs, fits the culture, and considers people's busy schedules. He has developed a series of 10 weekly encouragement and training letters, which he sends to new Christians, new members, and those rededicating their lives.

The Japanese and Chinese churches have home Bible study groups. The Japanese congregation says that they must become strong disciples for self-preservation because they are so few. Their goal is to know the Bible well lest they communicate their opinion rather than biblical truth.

Fellowship

Fellowship events in the Anglo church include potlucks and seasonal parties. Sometimes the potlucks are attached to a work party or are a joint event with the other congregations. They also provide weekly events for children and youth and monthly events for senior adults. A group meets weekly for prayer and monthly for lunch. A new women's ministry is planning retreats and other events.

The Korean congregation eats lunch together every Sunday. The pastor says they are a "first-century church"; they fellowship together, and they take care of one another.

The Japanese and Chinese congregations have monthly fellowships. They also have Gospel Home Bible Study groups. They meet in a neighborhood and network through family and professional relationships to establish relationships with new people.

The Japanese church has the unique fellowship of a cherry-picking outing. They go to a public orchard to pick cherries together and to meet other Japanese and to open doors for witnessing opportunities.

Ministry

Prayer ministry is the first mentioned—prayer meetings and prayer chains. The Korean church has a Korean language school with a goal to help the generations communicate. They also offer scholastic tutoring. Other ministries are accomplished with community and associational agencies, such as food and clothing ministries.

Worship

All the churches have strong music programs. The Anglo church has a drama team and a praise team that focuses on contemporary music. Pastor Knapp and the music director plan worship using different formats from week to week but always including a children's sermon.

For all of the congregations personal devotion is important. This is reinforced through their Sunday Schools.

The Korean congregation worships most often with daily services and two on Sunday morning. The Chinese worship service is the only bilingual service, though translators are available for any of the services. Midweek services meet at different times.

Results

The Korean church is growing rapidly, baptizing 25–30 this year. With their focus on prayer and discipleship, spiritual growth is also evident.

Although the pastor of the Japanese mission has baptized many people, the congregation remains small because so many return to Japan. Spiritual depth is evident in testimonies and commitment to evangelism and a Christian lifestyle. Some growth is evident. The new pianist is a teenage girl who was saved just two months ago. She worships alongside a 94-year-old woman who came to America years ago as a picture bride.

The churches are active in associational ministries. Ted Knapp and Peter Han hold associational leadership positions. Pastor Uchino is the SBC Japanese catalytic missionary in Los Angeles.

Chapter 5

CORINTH BAPTIST CHURCH

Chris Stewart is pastor of Corinth Baptist Church in Picayune, Mississippi. On a recent Sunday morning Chris led part of the service in a costume. It was family day following Vacation Bible School, and Pastor Chris went to change from his costume. When he got his Sunday suit back on, the pastor was standing at the back of the auditorium waiting for his next part in the service. While he was standing there, a couple walked in the back door.

It was clear from their clothes and demeanor that they were not accustomed to being in church. Since Pastor Chris was standing near the back door, the couple asked if he was the pastor. When he responded that he was, they poured out their problems. Pastor Chris felt led to minister to the couple immediately, so he took a few moments even though the service was continuing. The need was met, and one of the couple was saved the next day.

I tell this story because it demonstrates the way the people of Corinth work together as a team. While Pastor Chris was ministering, people from the church simply came forward to take care of the parts of the service the pastor would have done. They are a team. Pastor Chris Stewart said: "That's what makes this church special. Many are willing to step in and work hard to allow someone else to minister."

Corinth Baptist Church is located in a small town just out of Picayune, Mississippi. The people are in a lower income bracket, and the community has a rural feel. In the last few months, the average attendance at Corinth has increased from the mid 20s to more than 60. They baptized five last year and, as of this writing, expect to baptize eight new believers next month! As you would expect, there is a sense of unity and excitement.

Here are some of the concrete steps Corinth Baptist has taken to become a healthy, growing church.

Evangelism

Vacation Bible School is still one of the most effective evangelistic tools in the kingdom of God, and VBS is a major emphasis at Corinth. This year they started VBS on a Wednesday night and concluded with a family time on Sunday morning. One of the good things about this approach is that it encourages unchurched parents to come to church on Sunday and begin to get to know the people of the church.

I asked Pastor Chris how he gets the parents to come to the family time on Sunday morning. They start about a month before VBS with a letter to those who enrolled in last year's VBS. Later, teachers send letters to the parents sharing information about VBS. Church members work as a team to spread the word throughout the neighborhood.

Follow-up with those who make professions of faith is excellent. When a child makes a decision, the VBS worker who helped the child with the decision visits the home. The pastor and the Sunday School worker who would have that child if he or she enrolled in Sunday School go along on the visit. Often the pastor explains the decision of the child to the parents while the VBS and Sunday School workers work with the child.

Corinth Baptist Church plans a revival each year, and Pastor Chris feels it is one of the most effective evangelistic tools available. In addition, they have a block party that includes a free meal. They spread the word by going door-to-door in the community giving out tickets for the free meal.

Discipleship

Lots of Christian growth opportunities are available at Corinth. The church has a First Place group, and the youth are focusing on spiritual gifts. Adults are beginning a new study of ministry application.

The Sunday School is the centerpiece of the discipleship ministry. Corinth Baptist has an age-graded organization that provides a place for everyone to study the Bible in a group with whom they have something in common. Two new Bible study groups were started last year, and two more are planned for this coming year. Sunday School is so important that workers are asked to sign a worker's commitment. Pastor Chris said to his workers, "You are missionaries going on a mission." From the excellent work evident in the Sunday School, it's clear that the workers are on a mission. A mission to fulfill the Great Commission.

Fellowship

Fellowship activities at Corinth Baptist also accomplish the evangelism and ministry functions. For example, the monthly potluck supper provides wonderful fellowship for church members. The potluck also is an effective outreach because only 30 percent of the participants are church members. It is effective ministry because the program presents needed information such as how to use music therapy to alleviate arthritis pain.

Sunday School classes have fellowships designed to build team spirit and assimilate new members.

Ministry

One of the most effective ministries of Corinth Baptist Church is the marriage preparation classes done by the pastor. One couple, who were church members, resisted the idea of investing several hours in marriage preparation classes with Pastor Chris before their wedding. After he insisted and they came to the sessions, they were glad they had participated. In fact, they are now more active in the church than ever.

Worship

As in many smaller membership churches, Corinth Baptist's pastor, Chris Stewart, works with an all-volunteer worship leadership team.

Every Friday, when the music leader gets off work, he meets with Pastor Chris to plan the coming worship experience. They sometimes plan according to a theme, but they always plan something fresh to lead people into worship. Well-planned worship experiences are a key to warm, meaningful worship times.

Pastor Chris emphasizes that all church members should be participants in worship. The spectator mentality is discouraged. He reminds the choir that they are part of the leadership team.

When I sought permission to tell this story, Pastor Chris Stewart asked me to include this quote. He said: "I am blessed to be pastor of this church. Everything they have done has been their idea. God and the church have done it all. People express their dreams and ideas and work hard to see those things happen. It is a pleasure to serve as their pastor." A pastor with such a wonderful servant's heart must be an important key to having a healthy, growing church.

Chapter 6

RICHLAND BAPTIST CHURCH

Richland Baptist Church has a remarkable record for the last three years. During that time the church has grown in average attendance from 40 to 90. They have built a new building, using volunteer labor. They have participated in mission trips each year. And, while all this was being done, they have won and baptized 64 people with 72 other additions.

With all these accomplishments, it may surprise you to learn that Pastor Danny Jones is a bivocational minister. He does double-duty, serving as pastor and holding down a job at a shock absorber plant.

Time is always a primary concern for bivocational pastors. I asked Pastor Danny how he managed to find time to accomplish all those wonderful things during the last three years. First, Pastor Danny said he puts a high priority on preparing his sermons. No matter how busy a pastor becomes, a group of people at the church on Sunday need a word from the Lord.

Pastor Danny also reports that he "does his best" to make wise choices about his time. Most pastors must learn to choose the most important things from among many important things that demand our time. For bivocational ministers this is even more true. They have no time to do low-priority ministry.

Another way Pastor Danny and other bivocationals stretch their time is the participation of laypeople in the ministries of the church. The people of Richland Baptist have seen their pastor give sacrificially of his time. They have seen him set the pace by using his personal vacation time for mission trips. They have seen him work on the building every available hour. They have seen him come faithfully to Thursday night outreach even though he was there Sunday night and Wednesday night. This example of faithfulness seems to inspire some of the church members to be more faithful.

Bivocational ministers are an important part of God's kingdom work. They are gifted, talented people who lead some of our most effective churches. These double-duty ministers are not "part time." Just ask their families. They are full-time ministers who earn part of their income at a job other than the church. Bivocational ministers deserve our respect. Without their significant influence, many Baptists churches would have no God-called, effective pastoral leadership.

Here are some of the specific ministries Richland Baptist is doing to be healthy in fulfilling the functions of the church.

Evangelism

The visitation ministry on Thursday night is the key to evangelism at Richland. The pastor and a few faithful members knock on doors and tell people about the Lord and His church. They also visit the sick during this time.

The pastor describes himself as "having a heart for souls," and this shows in his preaching. Many of those who are saved in this ministry make their final decision and make it public as evangelistic sermons are delivered by Pastor Danny.

Two revivals each year help maintain a focus on reaching people for the Lord. This year Richland is joining other churches in the area in an area crusade sponsored by the association.

Discipleship

Sunday School and Discipleship Training are at the heart of this church's teaching ministry. The teachers are committed and work hard to fulfill the Great Commission.

Like thousands of other smaller churches all across the nation, Richland is using proven tools like Sunday School. This approach is simple, user friendly; and it is working.

Fellowship

Much of the fellowship of Richland Baptist takes place around the Sunday School and other Sunday activities. Special fellowship activities include a fellowship meal once a month on Wednesday night and a fourth Sunday night singing. They enjoy joining with other churches for fellowship in projects like the crusade sponsored by the association.

Ministry

Sunday School is also the primary ministry organization of the church. When a death or sickness occurs in the church family, people are mobilized to meet people's needs. The kinds of ministry range from a meal for a grieving family to help for stranded travelers. In every case the church is willing and ready to meet the needs of others in Jesus' name.

Worship

When Brother Danny stands to preach or lead some other part of the worship service, his people know he loves them. They know this because he has given them his most valuable possession before he even stands behind the pulpit. He has already given them his time in preparation, and that's a valuable gift.

Richland worship services are traditional, warm, and genuine. There is often appropriate humor. Many different people participate. Some sing special music; others play instruments or sing in the choir. There is a strong sense of family in the worship times.

Richland Baptist Church is an interesting and encouraging church. They are healthy and growing. Yet they have begun no really unusual, innovative approach. They plan well and use creativity in those preparations, but the approach is mostly traditional. This pastor and the church he leads just take simple, proven approaches and use them effectively.

The example of Richland Baptist Church and Pastor Danny Jones could be followed by thousands of smaller churches across the nation.

And if thousands of churches would follow this example, almost all of them would grow. This church is doing two essential things that God is blessing.

First, they are taking seriously their Great Commission mandate to reach the lost with the gospel of Jesus. They witness on Thursday night. Brother Danny preaches evangelistic sermons and leads the church in revival efforts. They go on mission trips. All this is to spread the gospel of Jesus.

Second, they do almost everything a church needs to do through their Sunday School. Discipleship, fellowship, ministry, and even evangelism and worship are part of a healthy Sunday School. Smaller churches can't, and probably shouldn't, have lots of different organizations to do their work. Most just need to use the existing Sunday School to its fullest potential.

The story of Richland Baptist is an encouraging story. It is encouraging because their success can be duplicated in many places. Take the Great Commission seriously and tell people about Jesus. Then use your Sunday School as the organization that mobilizes your church to healthy, balanced action.

Chapter 7

CALIENTE BAPTIST CHURCH

Caliente, Nevada, is a small desert town. One day, at a community meeting, a political disagreement occurred. Someone opposed a local politician. Even though everyone expected an angry outburst from the politician, it never came. Later the one who opposed the politician said: "The old you would have let me have it."

The politician replied: "I'm trying to live like a Christian, but I'm new at this. Don't push your luck." The politician and the town had been changed forever.

Another life was changed when a young man addicted to drugs became a Christian. His wife's mother was a bar owner in town. When she saw the change in the young man's life, she invited Jesus to be her Lord. The young man is learning to hold a job, be a husband and father, and be a Christian. Everyone in town knows he would be on the street or dead if he hadn't become a Christian.

Caliente, Nevada, is changing. The change began in the early 1980s. A small group started a church. They met first in the Oddfellows Hall, then in a storefront. Later, a woman donated land, and a work crew from Louisiana came to construct a building. In 1990, Russ Turner came from Las Vegas to Caliente and preached for the small congregation gathered there. After a few weeks, 18 members voted unanimously to call Turner to be their pastor.

He is an effective pastor and leader. He loves people. He has invested himself in this town. In fact, he is commonly thought of as the pastor throughout the community, even by those who are not members of his church. He has proven that he is a caring pastor and that the people of Caliente can trust him.

The leaders of Caliente Baptist Church understand that growth is a result of balance and health in the church. Smaller membership churches that grow are churches that are fulfilling the five functions in a healthy manner. Here are some specific ways Caliente Baptist Church is fulfilling the five functions.

Evangelism

As in all healthy, smaller membership churches, evangelism is done one person at a time. And when one life is changed, the whole community sees the miracle of that changed life. Whether the one saved is a local politician or a drug addict, changed lives are noticed in small towns.

Some might think evangelism is more difficult in a small town, and certainly small-town evangelism has unique challenges. There is also, however, a benefit to doing evangelism in a smaller church and town. When people get saved in a small town, everyone in town knows about it. A momentum builds when an entire town is talking about the miracle of changed lives. Because the leaders of Caliente Baptist Church are active in community life, they have a tremendous impact as "salt and light."

The Caliente Youth Center is a state-run juvenile detention center. The people of Caliente Baptist invest themselves in the lives of teenagers who come to their community because of past criminal activity. Church leaders built a relationship of trust with the administrators. This made it possible for the teenagers to attend services on Sunday. They have a Bible study time with other teens and participate in worship services. Because the people of Caliente Baptist invest themselves in these teenagers and faithfully witness of the power of Jesus to forgive and save, 15–18 teens from the Caliente Youth Center are saved each year.

In recent days, some have suggested that revivals are no longer effective for evangelism. This is simply not true. Caliente Baptist Church holds revival services each year, and people are saved every year. They work hard to make sure the entire town knows about the services and to present the gospel clearly. In fact, in a recent revival this small church had an average attendance of 145 each night during revival. A typical Sunday morning attendance is 50–75. Revivals are still an effective way to share the gospel.

Discipleship

I walked through the building used for Sunday School at Caliente Baptist Church. Even though there is much work yet to be done, Pastor Russ Turner is justifiably proud of recent improvements. The space is evidence of committed teachers and other workers who give of their time to teach people the Bible.

One of my earliest memories of Caliente Baptist Church is of a scene at Glorieta Baptist Conference Center, in Glorieta, New Mexico. The week had been devoted to training Sunday School leaders, and people had come from literally all over the country to take advantage of the excellent training. Following an inspirational evening service, I noticed a group of 20 or more people huddled together in the aisle. They were praying together and were obviously from the same church. Upon investigation, I discovered that these people were form Caliente Baptist Church. I was amazed to learn that a church averaging barely more than 60 in attendance could send more than 20 adults to Glorieta to become more effective Sunday School leaders. These dedicated people cared so much about teaching the Bible that they gave of their time and money to receive training.

Much discipleship is done one-on-one. When someone receives Christ under the ministry of Caliente Baptist Church, they are received into a spiritual family. Pastor Russ Turner thinks of many new converts as reclamation projects. The entire family takes responsibility for discipling the spiritual newborn.

Recently, 36 people studied *Experiencing God*. When church members use excellent resources like these, people will grow and become more like Jesus.

Fellowship

Being a part of Caliente Baptist Church is more like being in a family than doing church. That may be a valid comparison. Families have their ups and downs. They have disputes and conflicts, but those times are balanced with times of great unity.

Fellowship is more than cookies and punch. Caliente Baptist has fourth Sunday potlucks, and sometimes they invite other churches to join them for times of fellowship. But in addition to those fun times, the people of this church think of one another as family. They are brothers and sisters in Christ. Oneness in the body of Christ is the most important kind of fellowship.

Ministry

A traveler with car trouble asked a local bar owner about the availability of assistance. The bar owner said, "The Baptists will help you." Even though Caliente Baptist may not be able to help every stranded traveler, it is good to know that people in the community think of them as being willing to help. The church is active in helping others in Jesus' name throughout the community.

Ministry to the teens who pass through the Caliente Youth Center is a priority concern for the church. They provide Bible studies, youth activities, and much more for them.

Worship

The people of Caliente Baptist have been referred to as "happy Baptists." Their worship is a blend of hymns and choruses. They enjoy accompaniment by guitars and piano. People often feel free to clap along with the music.

Caliente Baptist faces a challenge in finding talented instrumentalists. They have learned, however, that worship can be exciting and meaningful in any size congregation.

Part 2

The Functions of the Church

Chapter 8

EVANGELISM

Evangelism is an essential function of the church. Any church that claims to carry out the Great Commission must be deeply involved in reaching people for Christ or evangelism. Mark 2:2-12 tells about four men who had a singular focus. They had a friend who needed to come to Jesus, and they overcame every obstacle and barrier to bring their friend to Jesus. That's what evangelism is. It's bringing people to Jesus.

Bringing people to Jesus can sometimes be hard work.—These men had to pick up their friend and carry him through the streets of the city.

My wife and I started a church in Northern California many years ago. One of the first things I learned was that bringing people to Jesus is hard work. We knocked on every door in that town. We witnessed and we prayed and we studied. But even hard physical labor was involved in the endeavor. I remember getting up early on Sunday morning and going down to the Veterans Hall where our church services were held and spending a couple of hours cleaning up and getting it ready for church on Sunday morning. Then we hauled in the pulpit and the guitar that we would use and all the hymnbooks and arranged all the chairs and made everything look as much like a church as we possibly could. Bringing people to Jesus was hard work.

Bringing people to Jesus is a team effort.—Perhaps one person could have physically carried the lame man through the streets of the city, but really four men were needed. Two men could have carried him fairly easily, but four men were needed to safely let him down through the hole in the roof. It was a job that required a team of four men. It's a joy to be a part of a Baptist family and to join with others in a team effort in bringing people to Jesus. Isn't it wonderful to know that thousands of missionaries are serving here in America and all across the world because we give and pray and focus on missions. It is wonderful to be a part of that team effort. It is wonderful to see thousands of young men and women trained in our seminaries. Isn't it wonderful to know that in your church are lots of different team members doing their jobs and carrying out their part of the team assignment in order to bring people to Jesus? Somebody has the building and grounds looking nice. Workers are driving up on Sunday morning with their arms full of teaching materials because they are members of the team, and they have prepared to teach their class and do a good job of sharing the Bible study with their classes. Bringing people to Jesus is a team effort.

Bringing people to Jesus will often meet opposition.—It should not surprise us to see opposition from the Pharisees, the hypocrites of the day. They opposed Jesus in everything that He did. But do you see in this story some opposition from the disciples of the Lord? Oh, they didn't mean to be the opposition. They didn't intentionally set out to stop anyone from bringing their friends to Jesus. But those disciples of Jesus who arrived early at the place He would teach and got themselves a good seat or a good place to stand in a doorway and then refused to give way when someone in need came at the last minute and tried to get to Jesus were part of the opposition. They did nothing more than stay in their comfortable place and listen to Jesus, but they were actually a part of the opposition. Someone standing in the doorway or someone with a good seat up front should have said: "Let's let these men in. They have a friend who needs to get to Jesus."

I wonder if in our churches we might be guilty of participating in this passive opposition. We might oppose people coming to Jesus by just finding a good position in the church and then refusing to be moved even when there is a need for us to move. Bringing people to Jesus will almost always meet opposition.

Bringing people to Jesus requires a creative approach.—They tore a hole in the roof. That was risky and expensive. They must have invested themselves somehow, either financially or in their time, in repairing the hole in the roof. It was unorthodox and unexpected; it was different from anything that had ever been done before. Bringing people to Jesus required creativity, and so it is today. If you want to be effective in bringing people to Jesus, you'll certainly be called on to use a creative approach. Sometimes you might need to invest a little bit more of your money or your energy or your time to bring people to Jesus. Sometimes you might need to do something that's unorthodox or different from what has ever been done before. But it's worth it because all around us are emergency situations. We are surrounded by people who must meet Jesus. Bringing people to Jesus requires a creative approach.

Bringing people to Jesus was noticed by Jesus.—Verse 5 has an interesting phrase: "When Jesus saw their faith, he said unto the sick of the palsy, Son, thy sins be forgiven thee." I expect that verse to say, "When Jesus saw *his* faith," with reference to the man who was healed. I believe that the healed man had faith; but according to verse 5, Jesus not only noticed and acknowledged the faith of the man who was lame, but Jesus also noticed the faith of four men who tore a hole in the roof and let their friend down at His feet.

You may serve in your church in a place where you receive little acclaim or notice. You may serve in a place where almost no one knows what you do in the name of the Lord. Let me say to you on the authority of the very Word of God that Jesus notices what you do in His kingdom. In 1 Timothy Paul said he had fought the good fight, he had finished the course, he had kept the faith, and henceforth he said there is laid up for me a crown of righteousness which the Lord, the righteous judge will give to me in that day.

And then Paul added something about you. Paul said, and not to me only, but also all them that love His appearing. Someday Jesus will reward you openly for what you have done in His kingdom. You are serving in a tough place. You are faithful in a difficult spot, but Jesus knows how faithfully you are serving, and someday He will reward you. Jesus always notices those who bring others to him.

Bringing people to Jesus results in changed lives.—Certainly the life of the man who was healed was changed forever. No more would he be carried by four of his friends. Instead he would walk out of that place a whole man, healed of his infirmity. But he's not the only one whose life was changed. The Bible tells us that all those who saw this miracle were amazed, and they said, "We have never seen anything like this."

Wouldn't it be wonderful if in your church this Sunday morning people went away saying, "We have never seen anything like that before"? Wouldn't it be wonderful if someone in your community were saved and changed so dramatically that the people all around your community said, "We have never seen anything like that before"? Bringing people to Jesus results in changed lives.

Any healthy, growing, smaller church must be serious about evangelism. The Great Commission is clear. We are to invest ourselves in reaching people for Christ. Here are some practical ideas to help you fulfill the evangelism function of the church.

Be Intentional

Evangelism is vitally important. Yet in spite of how often we speak of it, preach about it, or even train to do it, evangelism is often the task left undone. Be intentional about evangelism.

What has your church done in the past about evangelism? How effective was it? What could your church do this year to win people to Christ? Sit down with a few key leaders from your congregation and brainstorm answers to these questions. Come up with an evangelism plan for your church.

Model Evangelism

You, as a leader in your church, have a responsibility to lead out in evangelism. The pastor, of course, should set the pace in winning people to Christ. But all church leaders should obey the Great Commission. All church leaders should witness to others about Jesus.

Personal evangelism does not happen consistently without personal discipline. In 2 Timothy 4:5, Paul admonished Timothy to "do the work of an evangelist." That's a good word for smaller-church pastors today. Sometimes evangelism is work. Make personal evangelism the consistent, disciplined practice of your life.

Pastors, this Sunday morning, you will stand before your congregation and preach a message form God's Word. You will give an invitation at the conclusion of that message. Will anyone come forward in that invitation and receive Christ this Sunday? Will anyone come forward and make public a profession of faith made earlier in the week?

For many pastors the honest answer to these questions is, "I don't know." Many effective pastors, who take seriously their personal responsibility to fulfill the Great Commission and lead their people to do the same, make every effort to win someone to Jesus each week. To do this is not to be motivated by numbers. It is to discipline oneself to obey the Great Commission. Before invitation time this week, win someone to Jesus.

Preach Evangelistic Sermons

I am not suggesting that every sermon must be exclusively evangelistic. I would say, however, that every Sunday morning sermon and most Sunday night sermons should include a clear appeal for people to come to Christ.

A few weeks ago, I preached a sermon from John 21 about how Jesus restored Peter after Peter had failed the Lord. That sermon was primarily to the church. It addressed people who had failed the Lord and felt unusable in His work. As I made that main point in the sermon, I also reminded the congregation that this Jesus, who is so ready to restore us when we fail, is also ready to receive those who have never accepted Him. The Bible is about Jesus. He is found in every book of the Bible. Teach the Word faithfully, but make the connection to Jesus and invite people to accept Him.

One of the most important parts of evangelistic preaching is the invitation. A well-prepared sermon is incomplete until the invitation has been prayerfully and carefully planned. Plan the transition from the conclusion of your sermon into the time of commitment.

In *Invitation to Christ* by Wayne Bristow, we find some excellent help for preparing the evangelistic invitation. These ideas make lots of sense for smaller-church pastors.

Prepare spiritually.—God is surely dealing with someone who will hear your sermon. Certainly you will seek His guidance concerning the message. It is just as important to pray and seek His leadership about how the commitment opportunity will be presented.

Make the invitation clear.—Assume that people will be present who do not understand our Christian language. Even a child who is familiar with church talk may not really understand it. In fact, adults who have heard religious terms all their lives will find it easier to respond when clear, understandable language is used.

Tell people what they must know.—Near the conclusion of the message, restate the essential facts people must have to make an informed decision. If the message is evangelistic, state the essentials of salvation.

Tell people what action they should take.—If you want people to come forward during the singing of the invitation hymn and tell you about their decision or commitment, tell them so. Sometimes this is not as clear as we preachers think. For example, if the instrumentalists are playing softly, newcomers may not know whether to come during this soft music or to wait for the choir to sing again. Tell them what they should say if they come forward and "take you by the hand." Be specific.

Tell people what will happen when they come forward.—Present your invitation as if you were preaching to people who had never before been in a church service. If you or someone will pray with them at the altar, tell them so. If you will briefly greet them, and someone else will take them to an inquiry room (Be careful about using the terms *counseling* or *counselor*), let people know what to expect.

Give the invitation boldly.—Expect a response to the invitation. You are inviting people to Christ. You are inviting people to a renewed commitment to Him or to meaningful participation in His church. Clarify in your own thinking the invitation you are giving; then give it without hesitation or apology.

Prepare the people to expect and understand the invitation.—A public invitation to respond to Jesus is foreign to many who will hear your message. Make clear statements well in advance of actually offering the invitation. Consider a word of explanation in the bulletin or worship guide.

Use music appropriately during the invitation.—Use familiar hymns. This is not the time to learn a new text or tune. If choir or soloists are used, be sure not to draw attention to the person or persons singing. Prearrange signals for quick, clear communication between you and the minister of music.

Invite people to pray at the altar.—Invite your people to come forward for prayer during the invitation. Unless you use an inquiry room, consider praying at the altar with those who come forward. If you use the altar, others will feel more free to pray there. (If you are a single staff pastor, be sure someone else is available to receive those who come forward while you are praying at the altar.)

Personalize the invitation.—People come to Christ one at a time. Speak as if you were speaking to one person about Jesus. Ask the audience to listen as though you were speaking directly and exclusively to each of them.[1]

Establish a Prospect File

In the fall of 1993, as I began a new ministry through the Sunday School Board (now LifeWay Christian Resources), my family and I had a new experience. We prayerfully chose a new church home. My father was a pastor; my wife's father was a pastor, and I had served as a pastor for more than 18 years. The only way we had chosen a church was in the context of determining where God would have us provide pastoral leadership. When we found the community where we would live, we visited three churches. Representatives from each one came to our home, and we enjoyed all the visits. But one of the three did something that really set them apart.

The woman from the church knocked on the door. When we opened it, she introduced herself and said: "It was good to have you in our services last Sunday. I teach Preschool Sunday School, and I wonder if I might spend a few minutes with Katie." She spent the next 10 minutes with our daughter. She told Katie about the Bible story for next week. She told her who would sit with her and what games they would play.

When the woman left, my preschooler felt like the most important person in the world. She said, "Daddy, she came to see me."

The next day a worker from one of the children's classes called my son. He spent a few minutes on the phone with him, telling him about his class and encouraging him to come again.

Guess what. We went to that church the next week. In fact, we never visited another church. We joined in a few weeks.

This effective outreach was made possible because the church had a usable prospect file. These contacts would probably not have been made if Katie had been a note on my prospect card. The church had a separate card for each member of my family.

The master file should include each family of prospects. Be sure to get as much information as possible. In addition to the master file, use the pocket and card system as a working file. This system is designed to be kept in notebooks. In the smaller church, or the church with few prospects, begin with four notebooks. Use one notebook for preschoolers, another for children, one for youth, and one for adults. Even if some of these notebooks will be empty when you begin, label one for each age group. Ultimately, you will want one notebook for each class or department, but begin with one per age group.

Now you are ready to fill your prospect file. Be patient. A steady flow of new prospects is better than finding lots of prospects all at once. Schedule one prospect discovery project for each quarter of the year. Be consistent in getting complete information on anyone who participates in activities or ministries of your church. Remember to ask church members for names and addresses of people they know who need Bible study.

Many churches today use computers to manage prospect information. If you choose this approach, be aware of these factors.

The prospect assignment card or sheet you print should be easy to assign.—Giving a Sunday School teacher a sheet with 10 prospects on it means the teacher would have to cut it into strips to make an outreach assignment in class. Most teachers won't do this.

The prospect assignment card or sheet you print out should be designed with the expectation that it will be returned with a report of the visit.—Accountability is essential.

Get Names and Information from People Who Visit Your Services

It happens in smaller membership churches every week. The guest family arrives just as the choir is singing the call to worship. They slip in the door and sit on the back row. They leave quickly after (or sometimes during) the benediction, giving you and your congregation almost no opportunity even to say hello. Then they sometimes complain that your church isn't friendly.

How do you get enough information from that prospect to follow up effectively? In an age when many people desire anonymity, how do we get names, addresses, and phone numbers from people like these?

The basic principle is simple. Your guests are more likely to do what everyone else in the congregation is doing. If everyone fills out a card, they will likely fill out the card. If everyone else tears a tab off the bulletin, they will likely do the same. The best approach is a bulletin with a tear-off response tab. The next best choice is a guest registration card in the pew rack.

During the welcome time, ask everyone to tear off the tab.—The person welcoming the guests should have a bulletin in hand and tear off the tab before the people.

Invite all the people in the congregation, including guests, to tear off and fill out the response tab.

Emphasize communicating prayer needs with the response tab.— This will encourage regular attendees to fill out the tab and communicate vital prayer concerns as well. Church Bulletin Service Response Bulletins with response tabs, from LifeWay Christian Resources, include a place for prayer concerns. If you print your own bulletins, be sure to include this feature.

Reinforce the need for regular attendees to tear off and fill out the response tab each week.—The smaller the church, the more difficult it will be to get your people to do this. On occasional Sunday nights, talk with your people about the importance of everyone filling out the response tab. Remind them that guests are much more likely to give you the information you need if everyone fills out the card. Encourage them to communicate prayer concerns through this method.

Some people simply will not fill out a response tab.—Establish a welcome center and encourage the welcome center team to get as much information as possible.

Enlist a few friendly people to make their way to the exits during the benediction.—Train them to speak to guests and make them feel welcome. In the process, ask this team to get as much information as possible.

The smaller membership church is the most difficult place to establish good welcome procedures and keep them going.—The reason it is more difficult in the smaller church is that these churches often go several weeks without a guest. It takes real discipline to be ready for guests every week, when you only have guests every fourth or fifth week. Be ready for guests every week. Keep those guest-welcoming processes in place even when several weeks pass without a guest.

Train People in Evangelism

All Christians should know how to share their faith. The Great Commission commands us to make disciples in every part of the world. Why, then, are so many Christians convinced that witnessing is so difficult? Satan has deceived us. Christians have fallen for his tricks. Sharing your faith ought to be easy. In fact, if your experience with Jesus is genuine, telling someone about it is natural and normal. Remember, the Lord never commanded you to be like anyone else. Your testimony is your story. Witnessing is as simple as telling someone else about that which you have experienced yourself.

When I was 16 years old, in 1968, my dad helped me buy an old car. It took me 9 months to pay the $300 price of the car, but to me, that car was just about the greatest thing in my life. You know what I did? I did something natural and easy. I told all my friends (and most of my acquaintances) about my new car. I didn't need a training class. I didn't worry if someone would ask me hard car questions. I just talked about my car all the time because I was excited about it. A similar excitement about Jesus should result in a natural witness about Him.

I appreciate the value of witness training classes. I know that many people need help with developing a personal testimony that communicates with lost people. We sometimes complicate what should be simple.

One witness training approach that I have found helpful is built around two questions. The discussion around these questions provides an opportunity to deepen believers' understanding of exactly what happened to them when they were saved. It also provides an opportunity for participants to develop a personalized witnessing approach that describes, in words easily understood, a person's new birth experience.

What must a person know to be saved?—In most of the places I have asked this question, the discussion has produced a rather long list of answers. Some have suggested that you must know the Bible to be saved. Others say one must "really understand the meaning of forgiveness."

Soon the list begins to seem unrealistic. Someone may say, "I didn't know much about the Bible when I was saved," or, "I'm not sure I fully understand forgiveness now."

When it becomes clear that the list is much too long, ask: "What must a person really know to be saved? What did you know when you were saved?" Lead the group in a brief discussion of the few things one must really know to be saved. Although this article is not intended to be an exhaustive theological study, your short list should certainly include the following.

- You must know you have sinned.
- You must know who Jesus is.
- You must know how to receive Him as your personal Savior.

What must a person do to be saved?—In discussing this question, the trainees will be more careful what they put on the list. Insist that they use language a lost person could understand. Also make a distinction between actions that bring salvation and those that follow salvation. For example, someone will probably suggest that one must walk the aisle or be baptized to be saved. These are actions that come before or after salvation, but they do not answer the question, What must a person do to be saved?

Ask a few people to share what they did when they were saved. Gently insist that they identify those actions and put them in words a lost person could understand. If, for example, they say, "I gave my heart to Jesus," ask: "What does that mean? What did you do when you gave your heart to Jesus?"

Somewhere along the way, every person who has experienced new birth has talked to God. That prayer included a confession of sin, a request for forgiveness, repentance, and an invitation for Jesus to enter the person's life. Continue to probe gently until trainees can articulate their own conversion. Be prepared to share your own new birth experience in words a lost person could understand.

After a thorough discussion of what a person must do to be saved, invite participants to practice telling their own conversion stories to one another. Partners can help eliminate words lost and unchurched people would not understand.

Witnessing is as natural as a teenager telling his friends about a new car. Discussing these two questions can help Christians articulate their testimony.

Teach Your People How to Make a Visit

Outreach teams that Win: G•R•O•W is one of the finest outreach resources to be found. In it, author Jerry Tidwell provides some excellent tips on how to make a visit.

Set the time to go.—The ministry of visitation, if not planned, usually never happens.

Don't be pushy.—Leave the door open for future visits. Ask the person if he or she will allow you to come inside for a brief discussion about your church. Allow the prospect to make that decision.

Don't embarrass the prospect.—Generally, if the prospect is embarrassed by your conversation, you have not handled the visit properly.

Understand the principle of harvest.—Harvest will not come unless sowing and cultivation come first. The harvest may come several weeks after the initial visit.

Be clean and neat.—Dress casually. Let your dress communicate that the visit is important but not formal.

Go "two by two."—Follow Jesus' example recorded in Luke 10:1. Certain circumstances of the visit are more easily handled when two are present.

Be courteous.—If the prospect has company or is in the middle of dinner, the visitation team should graciously offer to come another time.

Don't be surprised by non-Christian behavior.—Remember, a change of heart will result in a change of behavior. Don't expect the change of behavior to occur first.

Avoid verbal overkill.—Don't use language the prospect won't understand.

Be complimentary.—Find something about the person, home, or children that you can honestly compliment.

Know names and family information.—Never carry the prospect assignment card to the door. Become familiar with it before you approach the home.

Decide who will lead.—One person on the visitation team should lead the conversation.

Go to the front door.—Don't assume the prospect will expect guests at the back door.

Pray for the person you are visiting.—Before leaving the parking lot at the church, pause and pray for the visitation encounter.

Prepare introductory remarks.—Without sounding as if the remarks are canned, state your name, your partner's name, and your church.

Show genuine interest in the prospect.—You cannot convey genuine interest without listening to the prospect.

Have a conversation plan.—Use the acrostic FORM.

> **F** stands for questions about *family*.
>
> **O** represents conversation about *occupation* or work.
>
> **R** is for the prospect's involvement in *religion* or church.
>
> **M** stands for your *message* or the reason for your visit.

If the visit is to a person who has a saving relationship with Jesus, focus on the church. Love your church and show genuine excitement about it.

If the visit is to an unsaved person, be sensitive to the leadership of the Holy Spirit. Ask for permission to share your personal testimony.

Plan Effective Revival Services

Revivals have played such an important part in the life of our country and in most of our lives that churches should make the revival meeting a priority. What steps are necessary to prepare for a successful revival? Salvation is of the Lord, and real revival comes from God; however, some steps are necessary to implement an effective revival meeting.

Plan well.—(Nothing is more important than prayer, but we'll deal with that later.)

- Establish the date for the meeting. Avoid calendar conflicts.
- Determine how long the revival will last. In the past, two-week revivals were common. Now three days is more common. The pastor should lead his people to have as long a revival meeting as possible.
- Decide the kind of revival your church needs. Does your church need spiritual renewal or an evangelistic harvest? What about an emphasis on the home or a Sunday School revival?

Enlist leaders.—One of the keys to successful revival is the selection of persons who will lead the meeting. The leadership of the Holy Spirit in selecting the preacher is absolutely essential. Make it a matter of prayer.

- Consider inviting a full-time evangelist at least once a year. Recognize that God has called some to be evangelists and use them in your church.
- Many times it is also wise to invite a music evangelist or minister of music to lead the revival music.

Include special features.—What are some ways to get people to attend?

Special night emphases can be helpful. Some special night emphases could be Children's Night, Youth Night, Men's Night, Women's Night, Neighbor Night, Family Night, Sunday School Night, Deacons' Night, or Old-Fashioned Night.

Ask someone to serve as chairperson for each special night. Let those chairpersons enlist others to help them on their assigned night. The more people involved in planning, the better the attendance.

Promote the revival.—Consider these methods:

- Revival posters
- Newspaper announcements
- Church newsletter
- Sunday School
- Prayer in worship services
- Word of mouth (This is most effective for lost people.)

Sow sparingly; reap sparingly. Sow bountifully, reap bountifully.

Discover prospects.—Begin with these:

- Prospects on the Sunday School roll
- Husbands, wives, or children of church members
- Your prospect file
- Visitors cards from your worship services

Always pray.—Revival cannot happen apart from prayer by God's people.

- Cottage prayer meetings are still effective. A leader should be enlisted for each home to bring a short devotion and begin the prayer time.

- Offer special prayer times at the church for your people to drop by and pray during the week.

Develop a 12-Month Outreach Plan

Here is a simple, three-step outreach process to help your church be intentional about evangelism.

Train your people in outreach.—At least twice a year, train your people in outreach. Excellent witness training resources can be found in *Outreach Teams That Win: G.R.O.W.* by Jerry Tidwell.[2] This resource also contains help for training your people to make a visit. Other resources are *Share Jesus Without Fear*,[3] and FAITH (a strategy for doing evangelism through the Sunday School).[4]

Plan and conduct four prospect discovery projects each year.—Once a quarter, do something intentional about finding prospects. Your total number of prospects should be approximately equal to your Sunday School enrollment.

- Register people who attend church activities and ministries, and get as much accurate information as possible.
- Do a bulk mail project targeted to some community near your church. Determine the demographic profile of those in the community. To what would they respond? If it is a community of young adults, perhaps they would like an audiotape of a Christian counselor talking about "Discipline in the Home" or "Preparing Your Preschooler to Succeed in School." If the community is filled with senior adults, they might be more interested in "Maintaining Health and Happiness During Retirement." Use the mailed brochure to offer the gift to those who return the post-paid response card or call the given number. Be sure the brochure is professional in appearance.
- Conduct a prayer needs search. Instead of a traditional survey, enlist a team of prayer warriors. Go door-to-door telling people about your new prayer ministry. Ask if they would like the prayer team to pray for them. Record the information, and pray for a week. Then return to the prospects and ask how they are doing. Caution: Really minister to them. Don't just use prayer to find prospects.
- Provide a bicycle safety demonstration for children in the neigh-

borhood. Ask the local police department to come and provide a safety presentation.

- Constantly search for new prospect discovery ideas. Talk with other pastors, attend conferences, buy books, pray. If you search and pray, you can find one good prospect discovery idea for every three months.

Plan and conduct four outreach participation events each year.

- Establish an outreach center. Using a table or bulletin board, make outreach assignments available after Sunday School and worship. Place the center in a busy area. Someone who is familiar with the prospect file should be there to help with assignments.
- Have a pie night. Ask members to make pies and deliver them to absentees. Offer to pray for them or take prayer requests back to the pastor.
- Have a Team Reach month. Announce that during Team Reach there will be several different ways for people to participate in outreach. Set up an outreach room with several kinds of well-labeled outreach possibilities. Include evangelism, absentee, ministry, newcomer, and hospital visits. Also invite people to participate in outreach by staying at the church to pray, make phone calls, or write cards or letters.
- Conduct a literature visitation project. Purchase some piece of literature for every member of your Sunday School. Label literature so that every member's name is on a piece. Ask teachers to deliver literature to the home of each member. If teachers cannot deliver all literature, enlist others to help. Remember, the purpose of literature visitation is not to distribute literature. It is to visit every member of the Sunday School.

---

[1] Wayne Bristow, *Invitation to Christ* (Nashville: Convention Press, 1998).

[2] Jerry Tidwell, *Outreach Teams That Win:G•R•O•W* (Nashville:Convention Press, 1997).

[3] Bill Fay and Ralph Hodge, *Share Jesus Without Fear* (Nashville: LifeWay, 1997).

[4] The FAITH Sunday School Evangelism Strategy is a cooperative evangelistic venture of the North American Mission Board and LifeWay Christian Resources. For more information about FAITH or to attend a FAITH training clinic, contact the Program Training Center at LifeWay, 1-800-254-2022.

Chapter 9

DISCIPLESHIP

Discipleship is an essential function of the church. *Discipleship* can be defined as one believer encountering another with the result that both are more like Jesus. With this definition, many church actions and programs would be included as discipleship. For example, Sunday School is discipleship because there many believers encounter one another in Bible study; and, as a result, they become more like Jesus as they study the Word of God. So Bible study is discipleship.

Discipleship Training is also discipleship. Churches today are doing Discipleship Training at all kinds of times and places.

Many other acts could be included in discipleship. When two neighbors sit down over a cup of coffee and talk about the Word of God, that's discipleship. When one teenager has a conversation with another at school about what they learned in Sunday School, that's discipleship.

Clearly, discipleship is an essential function of the church. In Deuteronomy 31:12, Moses gave some final instructions to the people of Israel. These were people he loved, and they had received the Law of God. Moses was giving some instructions to make sure the Law of God stayed on the hearts and minds and even on the tongues of the people of God. In that passage Moses said, "Gather the people together, men and women and children and the stranger that is within your gates, that they may hear and that they may learn and fear the Lord your God and observe to do the words of this law." This verse teaches us some important concepts about discipleship.

Discipleship begins with gathering people.—Our responsibility includes gathering people for discipleship and Bible study. Offering discipling or Bible teaching opportunities and inviting people to come is not enough. We must take the initiative to gather people to come and study the Word of God and become more like Jesus. It is our responsibility to find them and encourage them to come. We must provide a place and gather people to study God's Word.

Discipleship demands organization.—Deuteronomy 31:12 also suggests that when we gather people together we need to do so according to some organizational structures. The verse says "gather men, women, and children." Moses even said "and the stranger that is within your gates" In other words, make special provision for those that are different than us.

Let's be sure when we provide our discipleship opportunities that we provide for those who may be from a different place or speak a different language. Perhaps the differences are a little more subtle than that.

We should provide for people who are in a different socioeconomic level than most of the folks in our church. We need to provide for people from different cultural backgrounds. When we gather people to study the Word of God, when we gather people for discipleship, we need to be sure that we gather them in an organized way.

When we have a Bible teaching ministry, we ought to provide a place for anyone that might arrive at our doors. In the smaller membership church this can be a real challenge. Consider, for example, the smaller membership church with only one or two adult classes. They invite all adults to participate in one of those two classes. If this situation lasts many years, they will have adult mothers and daughters studying together in the same class. Clearly that's not the most ideal Bible teaching situation.

A new Bible study group that would address the needs of the younger folks would improve the ability of that church to reach and teach effectively. Organizing for discipleship is simply a way to gather people together according to their needs and distinctives. It is finding a place for them in Bible study where they can study with people with whom they have some things in common.

Discipleship includes hearing the Word of God.—Deuteronomy 31:12 goes on to say what should take place as we disciple folks. The first goal is to gather folks so they can hear the Word of God. There is value in simply hearing the Word of God. The Bible says of itself that it is "alive and powerful, and sharper than a two-edged sword." There is tremendous benefit to anyone just from hearing the Word of God.

People need much more than just hearing the Word of God, but it helps anyone to be exposed to the Word of God. If people come to your church and just hear the Word of God read aloud, they benefit from that experience. But Moses taught us to start by putting in place a strong foundation stone. That foundation stone is that people who come to the place of worship or to the house of God should have the opportunity to hear the Word of God. Disciple people by ensuring that they hear the Word of God.

Discipleship Includes learning from the Word of God.—Hearing the Word is not enough. In Moses' next step, he said we should gather people in order that they might learn. Hearing and learning are different, aren't they? It is possible for a person to hear and not learn anything. It is possible for people to hear and not really be impacted by what they hear. Therefore we need to teach the Bible. A healthy smaller membership church will provide discipleship ministries in such a way that, as people hear the Word of God, the Word makes a difference in their lives. They assimilate what they have heard. It becomes a part of their lives, and they begin to ask the question, "What does this have to do with me today?"

Sometimes a Bible study might seem to be merely a study of history, a study of something that happened in the lives of God's people a long time ago. The question might rightly arise: "That happened hundreds of years ago. What does this have to do with me?" Application needs to be made so that people can learn. Hearing is not enough. We need to provide discipleship opportunities in which people assimilate what they hear, take it into their own lives, and learn something about the Word of God.

Discipleship impacts our attitude about God.—The Bible continues to say that not only should people hear and learn the word of God, but they also should fear God. Fearing God is an interesting concept. When you lead people into meaningful Bible study, one of the results is that they fear the Lord.

What does it mean to fear the Lord? *Fear* has several meanings. Certainly to fear God means to have reverence for God. When people encounter the truth of the Word of God and are discipled, they ought to have an increased reverence for God Himself.

One of the ways that happens is that people see how far they fall short of God's glory. When I study the Bible, I see some of my own shortcomings. In the Word of God, I see the standard God has set for me. In the Ten Commandments, I see God's expectation of me. I also see the places and the ways and the times in which I fall short of God's standard, and that causes me to revere the God of heaven. It causes me to be in awe of the God who is so perfect and so majestic that He can provide this Word and set this standard.

Discipleship makes a difference in our actions.—Deuteronomy 31:12 concludes by saying not only should we hear and learn from the Word and fear God as a result of what we're learning, but we also should begin to observe to do all the words of the Law. Discipleship is not complete until the people of God begin to change their actions and their behaviors as a result of what they hear and what they learn.

It is possible for people to hear the Word of God and even learn something from the Word of God but be in such stubborn rebellion against God that they never change their actions or behaviors to reflect what they have learned. Discipleship should include such a profound and direct application to life today that the facts we have learned transform our lives. Studying the Word of God ought to make a difference in our actions and our behaviors.

Here are a few tips to help you carry out this discipleship function in a healthy manner in your smaller membership church.

SUNDAY SCHOOL

Discipleship includes Sunday School, but it is much more than Sunday School. It is impossible, however, to think of effective discipleship in a smaller membership church without beginning to think about the Sunday School organization.

Almost every smaller membership church has a Sunday School. If you don't have a Bible study organization like the Sunday School, you should start one right away. A Sunday School organization is the church mobilized to reach people for Christ and teach them the Word of God. A Bible study organization such as a Sunday School is the church fulfilling the Great Commission, and tremendous discipleship can be done through a well-organized Sunday School.

Let me give you a few tips about how to have a wonderful, effective, healthy, growing Sunday School in your smaller membership church.

Think of Your Sunday School Enrollment as a Ministry List

In a community like yours, there lives a young woman we'll call Amy. Amy's a single mom who lives in a mobile home. She works at Wal-Mart, making a little more than minimum wage. She has two children. Amy's daughter is an older preschooler, and her son is in first grade.

She worries about her son. He's having trouble in school. In fact, about once a week she has to take time off work and talk to the principal or his teacher because he's in some kind of trouble. They're beginning to wonder if maybe he has ADHD or some other such disorder. He has trouble sitting still and paying attention. She's concerned that he doesn't really have a positive male role model in his life since his father left the family.

Amy also worries about her little girl. Every day, when Amy goes to work, she takes the little girl by the day care center. She's never known of any reported abuse problems there, but it scares her to leave her little girl with people she really doesn't know.

Amy doesn't have the kind of network active church members have. She doesn't have any good friends, and she doesn't have any family close by. She really worries about her children and about the influences present in their lives.

One Saturday morning Amy was sitting on the couch folding clothes, and the children were watching Saturday morning cartoons. Amy looked at those cartoons, and she thought: *You know things have changed a lot since I was a little girl. These cartoon don't even look like they're fun, much less good for a kid.* But she leaves the TV on because at least the kids were quiet while they were watching. While she was sitting there folding clothes, she heard a knock at the door. It was Amy's neighbor.

During the conversation with her neighbor, Amy said: "I've been thinking about getting these kids into church. Don't you go to church somewhere?" She added, "When I was a child, my parents took me to church; and I think I ought to take my kids to church."

Amy's not a Christian. She doesn't have a church home. She simply recognizes that when her parents took her to church it did some good. She wonders if maybe her children are missing something because she's not taking them to church. So Amy said to her neighbor: "What about your church? Should we come to your church sometime?"

Amy's neighbor was excited about the idea of Amy's coming to her church, so she said: "Yes, in fact if you'd like to be a part of my Bible study group, I'll enroll you. My pastor was talking about this the other day. I'll get the addresses and birth dates on you and your kids, and I'll call the pastor. Everything will be arranged. We'll sign you up for one of our Bible studies." So the neighbor called the pastor, and the next day Amy was enrolled in Sunday School. Her children were enrolled in the appropriate preschool and children's classes.

The next day, the Sunday School workers were excited when they saw those new enrollment cards in their books. But you didn't think the devil was going to let Amy get away with this, did you? See Amy's a rookie. She doesn't know about getting kids ready for church. She's never done this before.

Amy got up that Sunday morning, and she looked around, and she thought, *Now what will these kids wear?* She figured that a little girl had to wear a dress to Sunday School, but Amy's little preschool girl never goes anywhere where she needs to wear a dress. Amy looked in the closet and finally found a dress. It was a little bit too small, but she thought it would be OK.

She didn't know that you're supposed to feed the kids breakfast and then get them dressed for church. She got them dressed first and then she sat them down to breakfast, and sure enough the little girl spilled chocolate milk all over the front of her dress. Now remember, Amy is not a Christian. She's not committed to the church, and so she said, "Aw, we'll go next week."

Next Sunday rolled around, and the little boy had a runny nose. He wasn't sick enough that she would have kept him home from school, but she didn't know if it was appropriate to bring a little boy with a runny nose to Sunday School. She only knew that she would be embarrassed, terribly embarrassed, if someone said: "Oh, you must take him home. You can't bring children in here when they are sick." So Amy decided to attend the following week.

When the next week came along, Amy went to visit her brother who lives about one hundred miles north of her community. So she missed Sunday School again.

Now it's been three Sundays since Amy enrolled in Sunday School. She still hasn't been to church. Back at the church, Sunday School teachers are looking at the Sunday School enrollment cards and beginning to think that Amy and her children aren't committed to the church or Bible study. People are saying, "If they were serious about Sunday School, they would have come by now; it's been three Sundays."

Amy is lost. She's not committed to Sunday School. She's not committed to the church. She's not committed to anything spiritual. She's just a person who said: "Yes, I'd like to be a part of your Bible study group. Include me." She put her name on the dotted line.

In most churches when a person doesn't attend Sunday School for two or three weeks, teachers will begin to think about dropping people like Amy and her children from the Sunday School roll. They do it in a lot of different ways. They might say to the pastor or the Sunday School director: "We have to get this Amy person off our Sunday School roll. Somebody enrolled her in Sunday School, and she has never once darkened the door of our church. She has no business being enrolled in Sunday School." And so they request that Amy be removed from the Sunday School roll.

Others approach this in a little bit different way. They take a pencil and write the word *inactive* across the card. They always use a pencil in case the person ever shows up, and for some reason they usually write it diagonally across the face of the card. Some would simply take Amy's card out of the book and move it to the back of the roll book.

Have you seen any of these things happen in your Sunday School? Why? Why would Sunday School teachers want to drop Amy from the Sunday School roll or move her to the back of the book or write the word *inactive* across the card that bears her name. Why do they want to do that? I think I know some answers. We want to drop people like Amy from their Sunday School rolls for several reasons.

First, Sunday Schools have an inappropriate emphasis on having 100 percent of the enrollment present. For years in churches I attended (and even pastored), we gave away 100 percent banners. This banner was given to the Sunday School class that had 100 percent of its enrollment present in Sunday School. The easiest way to get the 100 percent banner is to drop from the roll the people who don't attend. Awards like this have subtly encouraged teachers to drop people from the Sunday School roll when they don't attend. That's the worst thing a class could possibly do to get Amy and her family saved and to get them to attend Sunday School.

Second, members want to drop Amy from the Sunday School roll because her presence on the Sunday School roll reminds them of their responsibility to her. If she's enrolled in Sunday School, that means someone should be praying for her. Someone should be contacting her. Someone should be ministering to her.

Amy's name on the Sunday School roll reminds us that the class is failing to do what they ought to do about her and other lost or immature Christians who are enrolled in the Sunday School. I'm convinced that we should keep Amy and people like her on our Sunday School rolls. That's why churches should think of their Sunday School roll as a ministry list.

The Sunday School enrollment is a list of people who need ministry. Certainly that is true with Amy, and it's true of lots of other people in your Sunday School. There are some legitimate reasons for dropping people from the Sunday School roll.

1. Drop people from the Sunday School roll when they move away from the community.

2. Drop people from the Sunday School roll when they die.

3. Drop people from the Sunday School roll when they join or become active in another church.

4. Drop people from the Sunday School roll when they request to be dropped.

Classes ought to be aggressive in dropping people from the Sunday School roll when they meet one of those criteria, but in the absence of one of those four things, classes ought to keep them on the Sunday

School roll. Very likely if Amy and her children are dropped from the Sunday School roll, no one else will pray for them; no one else will minister to them; no one will visit them; and no one will reach them for Christ. Why not think of your Sunday School enrollment as a ministry list and keep Amy and people like her on that ministry list.

Someone has suggested that the best thing would be to include a person like Amy on the church's prospect list. That is inappropriate. Amy is more than a prospect. She has actually said, "Yes, I'd like to be a part of your Bible study group." She has signed up for Sunday School. She has agreed to be enrolled, and that makes her more than a prospect.

If Amy is moved to the prospect file instead of the Sunday School enrollment, she'll be contacted a time or two in the beginning weeks when she's initially placed in the prospect file. After that, she'll be old news. She'll be moved to the back of the prospect file, and no one will contact her any longer. Amy is ready to receive Christ. She is more than a prospect. She has agreed that she needs Bible study. Amy needs to be enrolled in Sunday School. Think of your Sunday School enrollment as a ministry list.

Use an Effective Process for Enlisting Sunday School Workers

In most smaller churches, the process for enlisting workers goes something like this. In late summer or maybe even early fall, the nominating committee has a meeting. They begin with a word of prayer at the beginning of the meeting, and then they start trying to link up names with the positions they have to fill. They really have started too late, so they don't have time to do it properly. They wind up enlisting people by buttonholing their friends and fellow churchmen in the hallways and saying: "Hey, remember that favor I did for you? Well, it's time for you to return the favor. We need a teacher for. . . ," and they tell the person where they need a teacher.

They may use a strategy in which the nominating committee member comes to the person who is being enlisted and says: "We need a teacher for this class. If you'll just take the class for a few weeks, we'll keep working until we find a teacher." Neither of those approaches is a good way to enlist Sunday School workers. Let me share a few ideas of how to enlist Sunday School workers effectively.

Pray.—In Matthew 9:36-38, Jesus instructed us to pray that the Lord of the harvest would send laborers into His harvest. Notice that the fields belong to Him, the harvesters are His laborers, and the harvest belongs to Him.

When we undertake to enlist Sunday School workers, our task is to find the one person in our church that God would have serve in each position. The nominating committee, or whatever group will be doing the enlisting, should meet early in the process.

If your new church year begins in September, then you should begin to meet in late spring or early summer. This will give you time to pray about God's will concerning the positions you'll be inviting people to fill.

I suggest that every member of the enlistment team or nominating committee take a certain number of the positions to be filled and agreed to pray every day for a week about the one person God would have serve in that position. The prayer should go something like this: "Lord, who is the one person in all our church that You would have serve in this position?" When the nominating committee or enlistment team approaches its task with that kind of a prayerful manner, then God will surely honor their efforts.

Make a list of needed workers.—Don't take a shortcut at this point. Actually make a list of the positions to be filled. If your work is primarily focusing on Sunday School, this should, of course, include all the Sunday School leadership team; and it should include the teachers in every class. In some churches it should also include an outreach leader for every class or department.

Make a list of potential workers.—Put the list on paper. That list of potential workers should contain the names of every person in the church who is a potential teacher.

Many times at this point, when committees consider potential workers, they make some tragic mistakes. Some nominating committees eliminate people before those people have had an opportunity to consider whether they should lead in the capacity being considered. For example, the committee is looking for a teacher for a preschool class. Someone suggests the name of a person in the church. And then someone else on the nominating committee says: "Oh, he wouldn't do it. We asked him last year, and he turned us down."

Now what the committee has done in that instance is to say no for a person who should have had the opportunity to consider whether he will serve. Remember that the task of the enlistment team or nominating committee is to ask God for the name of the one person in all the church that He would have serve in that position and then go to that person and properly, effectively share information about the job and attempt to enlist him or her.

Don't say no for people who might be considered as potential workers. If the person considered is capable of serving—that is, he or she has the abilities needed to serve and if he or she would be acceptable to the church, then put that name on the list of potential workers. Do not leave people off the list of potential workers because they said no in the past or because someone on the committee thinks they would be unwilling to serve. No one really knows about their willingness. Consider only whether they are capable of serving and whether they would be acceptable to the church. If both those questions can be answered in the affirmative, then put those names on the list of potential workers.

Make a list of training opportunities.—At several places in this process a committee may be tempted to take shortcuts. This is one of those places.

Nominating committees or enlistment teams may be saying to people they are enlisting: "We have lots of training available. If you will accept this position, I assure you that there are training opportunities."

Training opportunities need to be put in print and left in the hands of the person you're enlisting to lead or teach. Putting the actual training opportunities with dates and the times. On this list of training opportunities be sure to include national training events, such as conferences offered at Ridgecrest and Glorieta, training events sponsored by your state convention, training events sponsored by your local association, and training events sponsored by your local church.

If your church is not in the habit of providing training opportunities, begin to provide at least one training opportunity for Sunday School workers every year. Schedule it, determine the time when the meetings will be held, and put that training opportunity on a list that you can leave with the potential worker.

Pray again.—The nominating committee needs to pray throughout the enlistment process. With the list of potential workers and the list of positions to be filled, pray the simple prayer again that you prayed in the beginning of the process. "Lord, who is the one person in all our church that You would have serve in this position?"

Decide on one person.—Many nominating committees determine the person they will ask to serve and select a backup in case their first choice turns them down. The only reason for backup names is that the committee started the process too late. When someone says no, the committee doesn't have time to pray again: "Lord, this person turned us down. Who is the one person now that You want to serve in this position?"

Determine which person you feel God would have serve in the position and enlist that person. Do not have a backup name, but decide on only one person for each position.

Make an appointment.—You know that place in the sermon when the pastor says, "If you forget everything else I say today, remember this." We're at that point in this procedure for enlisting Sunday School workers. If you forget everything else about enlisting Sunday School workers, remember and implement this. Make an appointment to enlist Sunday School workers. Decide as a committee or as an enlistment team not to enlist Sunday School workers in the hallway or in the church parking lot. Do not minimize the work of your committee or team by buttonholing someone haphazardly.

What is communicated when a committee member enlists someone to teach a Sunday School class by saying, "We've been meeting as a nominating committee, and I've been meaning to talk with you about teaching this class." This approach communicates that the class the person is asked to teach is not really important. The job they're asked to take is unimportant. It is not even important enough for an intentional conversation about enlisting them to serve in the position.

Make an appointment. Perhaps the appointment could be held at the church, in the room where the class would be taught. Enlist the person in that very room. If that's not possible, arrange to visit in the person's home or place of work. Call potential workers on the phone or see them at church and make an appointment for a specific time set aside just for the enlistment process.

Make the enlistment visit.—Explain the selection process. If the committee prayed, sincerely prayed and sought the will of God concerning that position, and if God has led the committee to speak to that one person about teaching this Sunday School class, say, "We have prayed, and we feel led to invite you to teach this Sunday School class."

Note this carefully. I do not suggest that you say "We have prayed, and we feel it is God's will for you to teach that class." You don't know that. You do know, however, if you've prayed sincerely, that God has led you to speak to that person.

During the enlistment visit, explain the expectations of the responsibility. For example, if the Sunday School organization has a worker's covenant, share that covenant with the person. If you have job descriptions or position responsibilities for the classes, share that in printed form with the person. If the church expects teachers to participate in outreach, to be well prepared, or to arrive 15 minutes before the class begins, explain these expectations. In fact, those expectations should be put in writing and left with the person.

When you enlist a person to serve as a Sunday School teacher, you ought to leave with the person all the resources for teaching that Sunday School class. Provide a teacher's book, a resource kit, and a member's book. Open that resource kit and that teacher's book and show the potential teacher how to prepare lessons. This requires a little bit of homework on your part as an enlistment team; but your presentation may impact the decision.

If you simply say: "Our materials are easy to use. I'm sure you can do it," the worker may go away from the encounter thinking, *I don't think I can do this.* Presenting the teaching materials and showing the potential teacher how to prepare can leave the potential worker with a strong sense that he or she could lead that class if led by the Lord.

Also during this time of the enlistment, share the list of training opportunities. Then ask him or her to pray about the possibility.

Start the process early enough so there's enough time for potential workers to pray. Allow one week for them to pray about this important matter and then contact them again.

Making an appointment for the response is probably unnecessary, but follow up intentionally. A phone call will allow them the opportunity to respond to the invitation to teach that class. It is best not to receive their response in the hallway at church. They may want to ask some additional questions, or they may feel a need to share some embarrassing or private issues about why they're not taking the class.

If you will use this simple procedure for enlisting your Sunday School workers, you will likely find all the workers God has for your church. Many times pastors and Sunday School workers say: "You just don't understand our situation. We don't have enough workers." That may be, but f you sincerely pray and if God lays somebody on your heart, you ought to talk to that person. If you use shortcuts in this process, you'll cut the effectiveness. If you'll do this process in its entirety, you'll have the best opportunity to find all the workers God has for your church.

Provide Training Opportunities for Sunday School Workers

Every Sunday School worker needs training—even those who are experienced. They may have been teaching Sunday School for many years. They know how to teach the Word of God. But all Sunday School workers need refreshing. They need to encounter fresh ideas. They need to become aware of changes in curriculum and methodology.

All Sunday School workers can learn something new. All Sunday School workers can find new ideas to reenergize their ministry. All Sunday School workers need training.

Some of your Sunday School workers will go with you to Ridgecrest or Glorieta if given the opportunity. Many of your Sunday School workers will go with you to a state or associational training event. But some of your Sunday School workers will do neither. Some of them will only participate in training if you offer that training at your local church. For those individuals schedule some kind of training opportunity at your church.

Be intentional about training. Give all your workers a list of training opportunities. Include national, state, associational, and church training opportunities for the coming year. Make Sunday School workers aware of training opportunities for individual study. Here are some examples of individual and small-group studies that may be effective in your church.

Age-group workers agree to read a book by a given date.—On that date the workers meet together and take one or two hours to complete the Personal Learning Activities for Christian Growth Study Plan credit.

Directed reading is an approach in which workers agree to read specific books during a set period of time.—For example, workers might agree to read one book a quarter. If all the workers in an age group are reading the same book, plan opportunities for purposeful discussion of the materials they are reading.

Wednesday nights are a good opportunity for training Sunday School workers.—During weekly workers meetings and following the midweek service on Wednesday night are prime opportunities for training. Leaders might ask workers to read one chapter a week in a book in order to have a brief discussion during their worker's meeting.

The pastor might use the midweek service to teach a Sunday School leadership training book.—Often such a study is helpful for all Sunday School leaders and of interest to all church members, training some as potential workers and leaders..

Some Sunday School workers prefer to do their training on an individual basis.—Encourage these workers to take a book, study it, and answer the questions at the end of each chapter in order to receive Christian Growth Study Plan credit.

Involve Workers in Planning

A Sunday School team needs to be involved in planning meetings. For some churches meeting on a weekly basis is just right. Other churches prefer to meet monthly. But every church, including smaller membership churches, needs to gather to plan the work of the Sunday School. If you have no Sunday School worker's planning meeting, when do your workers have an opportunity to pray together about Sunday School concerns? If you have no Sunday School workers meeting, when do your Sunday

School workers plan the work of the Sunday School? Whether monthly or weekly, your workers need to be involved in planning the work of the Sunday School.

Develop a 12-month Outreach Plan for Your Church

In order to have an effective Sunday School in the smaller membership church, every church needs to have an intentional approach to outreach. This subject is dealt with in depth in the chapter on evangelism. Remember to include in your evangelism plan an annual event to find prospects. Do something intentional about involving your people in outreach, and do something intentional about training your workers in witnessing and in visitation.

Set and Reach an Attendance Goal on High Attendance Day in Sunday School

A high attendance day can provide a needed boost for your Bible study ministry. It can lead your people to focus on a common goal. A high attendance day can bring a sense of excitement to your entire church.

Here is a simple process for using the high attendance day to boost involvement and enthusiasm in your Sunday School.

Set a date.—The date is important. Choose a time when the calendar is clear of other priority emphases. Avoid holidays. Some churches prefer to link this date with naturally high-attendance times (like Easter), while others see the wisdom of attacking those traditionally low-attendance times like midwinter or summer slump. It is really encouraging to have an all-time record high attendance in Sunday School in the middle of what would have been a summer slump. This approach also has the added benefit of an accompanying boost in activity and attendance before and after the event.

Set the goal.—Be careful. If the goal is too high, people will be frustrated and discouraged. If it is too low, they will not be challenged. A few more than ever before is usually a good idea. Participation is best if the entire leadership team, including teachers, sets the goal.

Six weeks before the big day, publish the first weekly countdown bulletin.—This brief newsletter is for teachers and other leaders. At the top, place the theme of the high attendance day. For example, if your event is near Valentine's Day, you may consider "Put Your Heart in the Church Day" for your theme. Then list the actions leaders should take on that day to prepare for the event. Distribute a countdown bulletin each week until the event. Here are a few examples of items that might go in a countdown bulletin.

- Lead your class in praying that God will use Put Your Heart in the Church Day to reach people for Christ and to involve them in life-changing Bible study.
- Set attendance goal for your class.
- Discuss ways your class can help publicize Put Your Heart in the Church Day.

Three weeks before the high attendance day, send a personal, hand-written invitation to all Sunday School members and prospects.—Print out names and addresses of all members and prospects in groups of 10.

Place each list, consisting of 10 names and addresses, in a large envelope. Also place an instruction sheet, a sample letter, a pencil, and 10 sheets of stationery or note cards, and 10 church envelopes in the packet.

Place the packets, each containing everything needed to write 10 letters, on the Lord's Supper table. Enlist members to take the packets home and handwrite the letters. Remind them to hand address the envelopes and bring the completed packet back to the church the next Sunday. It is best to mail all packets at once from the church.

Two weeks prior to the high attendance day, contact all members and prospects by telephone.—Use a process similar to ththat for sending written notes, but in each packet place the names and phone numbers of 10 members and prospects and an instruction sheet to equip your people to make the calls.

The week before the high attendance day, schedule a visitation blitz.—Have outreach blitz activities at least three times during the week—one during a weekday morning, one for a weekday night, and one on Saturday morning.

When the big day comes, celebrate the victory. Brag on all the classes and departments that meet their goals. Enjoy the day.

Develop a 12-month Training Plan for Volunteer Workers

Training should be a lifelong pursuit for people who serve God through the local church. Even those who have many years of experience can gain new insights and benefit from new approaches. Here are a few ideas to get you started with a training plan.

Enroll workers in the Christian Growth Study Plan.—Even those who have not participated in training in the past and are not currently participating will benefit from enrollment. Enrolling all workers will make it possible for you, as a leader, to track the training progress of your team.

Make a list of available training opportunities.—Include the following:

- National training opportunities (Glorieta and Ridgecrest)
- Training offered by your state convention
- Training offered by your association
- At least one training event offered at your local church
- Individual training opportunities designed for self-study

Provide this list to all workers as they are enlisted. Also use the list to offer training options to workers throughout the year.

Determine which training opportunities you will lead your workers to attend.—Giving consideration to the needs of your workers, times training will be offered, distances to be traveled, etc., decide which training events on the list you will emphasize.

Determine the training opportunities you will offer at your local church.—If the state convention is offering an excellent training event on evangelism through the Sunday School and many of your workers will attend, you should probably choose something else to offer at your local church. You may choose to offer something to help workers understand the characteristics of the age group with which they work.

Calendar at least one or two training events at your church.—Give training a priority in your calendar. Select a time without conflict on the calendar. Remember to budget needed funds. Your associational ACTeam will probably be happy to help.

Encourage workers to use individual and small-group studies to continue work toward their Christian Growth Study Plan Diplomas.

- Ask workers to read one chapter every week in a good training resource. As them to report and discuss what they've read during your workers planning meeting.
- Make books and tapes available, from the church media library, to workers for home and individual study.
- Invite a group of workers to cooperate on completing a training book. A different member of the group can focus on each chapter and complete the study questions at the end of that chapter. Then the group can come together for chapter reports. Remember, each person should read the entire book.

Publicly recognize workers who have earned leadership diplomas.— Take time during a Sunday morning worship service to tell the congregation about the excellent work done by some church leaders. Tell of the hours they have invested in making themselves better teachers or leaders. Present diplomas or nice certificates. Another way to recognize workers is to have a worker appreciation banquet at the end of the church year. Some smaller-church pastors have even prepared the meal themselves. Make volunteer workers feel important and appreciated.

Begin New Bible Study Groups

One secret to Sunday School growth is to start new Bible study groups. After about 18 months Bible study groups usually reach their maximum attendance. The people in those groups get to know one another and relate well to one another and are simply not focused on reaching new people for Bible study.

Groups are interesting. People get comfortable in a group. They know all the people. They know where they are going to sit. They know who speaks up and who doesn't. They know who will read aloud or lead in prayer. A group can become comfortable. When people come to Sunday School, they are part of a group and in that group are strong relationships. Favors have been done for one another; ministry has been done for one another; prayers have been uttered for one another. All of that is an important part of the strong relationships that exist in a group.

To encourage growth.—When I go to Sunday School on Sunday morning, I sit down with a group of men who know me and who have prayed for me and who have ministered to me. When a newcomer comes into our Sunday School class, we welcome him into our group. We want him to feel a part of the group. But the newcomer doesn't know about the prayers we have lifted up for Ted's sister who has cancer. They don't know about the time we ministered to John and his family as he was dying. Breaking into an existing group is difficult.

It a simple fact of group dynamics that new Sunday School groups, new Bible study groups, grow faster. It's easier for a newcomer to break into a new group than it is for a newcomer to break into an existing group. Of course, some people can join a group and instantly become a part. But many people in our society feel like outsiders. Even though we make them feel welcome, we are prepared for their arrival, and we have a book to put in their hands, newcomers to the group are really outsiders.

When we start a new Bible study group, we provide an opportunity for those people to be involved in a new group. It's much easier for them to be assimilated into that group. Take a look at your Sunday School organization. Do you need a new Bible study group or two?

To make room for more people.—Consider starting a new Bible study group when your room is full. Be careful about this. Take a large room and put a table in the middle of that room. Put chairs around the table. The room is full when the table is full. Even though the room might have a capacity of 20, if there are eight chairs around that table, the room is full at 8 and not at 20.

When you consider whether your rooms are full, remember also that generally 80 percent capacity of a room is full. If a room has 10 chairs, you likely will not average 10 in attendance in that room. When people come into a room and sit down, they often put their Bible or purse in the next chair. They move the chairs around to get comfortable. When people come into a room where every seat is taken, they may subconscious tend not to come again. The subconscious mind says, *They will not really notice if I'm not there because the room is full anyway.* So it is best to consider a room full at about 80 percent of its actual seating capacity.

To meet a need.—Another occasion for starting a new Bible study group is when you see a group of people in the community who need ministry or Bible study. The community in which we live has a new group home for mentally retarded adult men. Our church saw a need for Bible study in that group, and we started a Sunday School class just for men from that group home and some of their friends and acquaintances. We identified a group in our community that needed Bible study and ministry, and we started a new class to provide that Bible study and ministry. Your community may have a group of senior adults, young adults, or teenagers who need Bible study and ministry. You may have a group of parents without partners or a group of grandparents or retirees who need Bible study and ministry. Start a Bible study group with that group especially in mind.

To extend ministry to members.—Also, consider starting a new Bible study group when your existing groups exceed the ministry capability of the class. Sunday School is about more than just teaching the class on Sunday morning. Ministry should be taking place in that Bible study group. For example, let's say you have a Sunday School class in your church that has 15 people enrolled with an average attendance of 8–9. You might look at that enrollment of 15 and think: *Surely that class has room to grow. Only 8–9 of the 15 enrolled attend. That's below the enrollment ceiling. They don't need a new Bible study group.*

That may not be true. If the teacher of that Bible study group travels during the week and has no time to minister to the 8–9 people who attend much less the 15 enrolled, then perhaps you should consider starting a new Bible study group. That class has exceeded the ministry capability of its class.

On the other hand, you may have a class that's a little bit larger than the commonly accepted enrollment ceiling of 25 for an Adult Sunday School class. That class may be able to go a little bit larger because the teacher has plenty of time for ministry and is willing and able to minister, not only to the members but also to prospects.

When you determine that you need to begin a new unit, be careful not to split an existing Sunday School class. The object is to create a new unit and leave every other existing class as strong and healthy as possible. Do not divide a class in half and essentially create two new units. Instead, enlist a leadership team—including a teacher, someone to deal with outreach, and two people to deal with caring ministries—to be the nucleus of the new class. The teacher and the outreach leader may come from an existing class, but the care group leaders may come from another part of the Sunday School organization. Carefully and prayerfully enlist the leadership team for the new Bible study group without damaging existing Bible study groups. Ask members of existing Sunday School classes to think of themselves as missionaries or as those sending missionaries. Invite them to participate in starting the new Bible study group as a missionary or ambassador from the existing Sunday School classes. Some may wish to help the new class for one year, then after that period of time to return to the existing class.

DISCIPLESHIP TRAINING AND OTHER APPROACHES

Sunday School is an important approach to discipleship, but it is not the only approach. Many churches today, including smaller membership churches, have some of the most effective Discipleship Training ministries in the history of the church. The resources available for discipleship are unparalleled. Resources available today can help your people with every need that might arise in their Christian life. Many churches still enjoy, appreciate, and use a strong Discipleship Training ministry that meets on Sunday night at the traditional time. If this is true of your church, thank the Lord and use it in a powerful and wonderful way.

Other churches are using a variety of approaches to carry out the function of discipleship in their churches. People gather in small groups in homes in different parts of their communities to study excellent resources. The opportunities are as varied as are the people and needs involved. Discipleship takes place at all times of the day and at all places in the community. This is a wonderful time for smaller membership churches to step up to the plate in discipleship and provide the best in resources and training for discipling ministries.

Carry Out the Discipleship Function in Your Preaching

Pastors of smaller membership churches have a opportunity to do discipleship in the church through their preaching. More than anyone else in the church, you have the ear of your people. Many times on Sunday night and Wednesday night, your people will enjoy a verse-by-verse study through a book of the Bible. They would benefit tremendously from an in-depth study, and they would become more like Jesus as they encounter the Word of God through your preaching and teaching. Take full advantage of the preaching opportunities to do discipleship in your church.

Carry Out the Discipleship Function Through the Families in Your Congregation

Equip the families in your church to disciple their own family members. Provide people the encouragement and the opportunity to begin a family daily devotional time. Encourage them to read the Bible daily and to tell Bible stories to their children and to make that a special time. Children are discipled more at home than anywhere else. What a joy it is to see godly Christian parents raising their children in the nurture and admonition of the Lord, making disciples of their children as they pray for them and with them, as they read and study the Bible together, and as they share Bible stories with them. Encourage your families to take responsibility for discipleship.

Mentoring Is a Way to Carry Out the Discipleship Function of the Church

Mentoring takes place when two believers come together and one shares a wealth of experience with another who may not be as experienced. Paul was a mentor to Timothy, and both benefited from the relationship. What a joy it is in the church to see experienced believers, mature disciples, take new believers or disciples who might be less mature and teach them some of the things they know and help them to understand some of the Scriptures they are studying. It's a joy to see them sitting together in church, to see them praying together and working with each other in the church.

Mentoring relationships are usually initiated by the less experienced person, the less mature person coming to a mature believer to seek a mentoring relationship. Most mature believers are humble enough that they would not think of going to an inexperienced or immature believe and saying: "Listen, I have some things to teach you, so I'm going to mentor you. If you do what I tell you, then you will be all right." However, the mature believer will respond when approached by the immature believer or the inexperienced disciple who says: "I see something in your that I'd like to develop in my own life. Would you invest some time mentoring me? Would you help me to become a stronger disciple, to become a more mature part of the family of God?" Both members of a mentoring relationship grow. The mature believer may again become aware of basic truths as those are shared and recapture the salvation joy of the new believer. The new believer gains valuable insights and the benefits of experience. You, as the leader of a smaller congregation, can often facilitate mentoring relationships as you match interests or needs among mature and immature Christians.

Chapter 10

FELLOWSHIP

Fellowship is an essential function of the church. If a church is to be healthy, balanced, and growing, it must be involved in fellowship. But fellowship is more than cookies and punch.

A few weeks ago a friend and coworker stopped me in the hallway at LifeWay Christian Resources and asked me about a member of my family who was going through a health crisis at the time. As I shared with him, he put his arm around me and prayed for me. He prayed that my family member would be well and that I would be blessed during this time when I needed a friend and the Lord. When Bob prayed for me, he was involved in a fellowship ministry.

Fellowship is much more than believers getting together and having a good time with fun, conversation, and refreshments. Fellowship oftentimes involves one believer getting under the load with another believer—one believer helping another by walking alongside in a way that helps share the load.

In 1 Corinthians 12:12, Paul taught the Corinthians about fellowship. He said, "For as the body is one, and hath many members, and all the members of that one body, being many, are one body; so also is Christ." In that verse Paul taught an important lesson about fellowship. The church is the body of Christ. And even though there are many members in the body, we are still one body. That which we have in common in our relationship to Jesus is more significant than anything that might separate us.

Perhaps you've had the experience of traveling to a new place and meeting a believer. Even though you've never met before, you instantly have something powerful in common with that Christian brother or sister. There is a bond between you. That bond is what you have in common in Jesus. You might be of different cultures and backgrounds and lifestyles; but if you have in common a relationship with the Lord Jesus Christ, you are a part of the body.

A local New Testament church is one body. It has many members, and those members are different from one another. Each is unique, but together they are one body. That has some significant implications, doesn't it? It means that whether we try to help or hurt one another, we are one body. It means that even if two parts of the body move in different directions, they are still unalterably, unavoidably one body. Fellowship means we recognize that even though we are many members we are one body.

First Corinthians 12:13 says, "For by one Spirit are we all baptized into one body, whether we be Jews or Gentiles, whether we be bond or free; and have been all made to drink into one Spirit." In this verse Paul emphasized that even though we are different we are still one body. We share something in common and that something is the presence and power and filling of the Holy Spirit of God.

Paul recognized that Jews and Gentiles were as different as they could be. Their customs, their habits, their ways of approaching life were very different from each other. Yet Paul reminded them that they had in common the presence of the Holy Spirit. Since the Holy Spirit lived in both Jews and Gentiles, Paul was suggesting that what they had in common was more significant than all the differences that come from being Jew or Gentile.

Paul also pointed out in verse 13 that some of them were slaves and some were free. Can you imagine that? Slaves and free people were worshiping together in the same church. They came from very different situations, but they had something in common that was more significant even than whether they were slave or free. They had in common the presence of the Holy Spirit of God. You are one body, and you have in you one Holy Spirit of God.

In verses 14-18, Paul said: "For the body is not one member, but many. If the foot shall say, Because I am not the hand, I am not of the body; is it therefore not of the body? And if the ear shall say, Because I am not the eye, I am not of the body; is it therefore not of the body? If the whole body were an eye, where were the hearing? If the whole were hearing, where were the smelling? But now hath God set the members every one of them in the body, as it hath pleased him."

Those verses are filled with meaning about fellowship in the body of Christ. Paul was suggesting that every member of the body is important. If you liken your church to a body, could you identify some people who would be like the feet? They are humble. They never get much acclaim or notice, but they carry the load. Every time something needs to be done, you can count on them. They just keep pressing on. They are like the feet in the body.

Perhaps others in your church are like the eyes or the ears. They are sensitive to the needs of those around them. They see what's happening in people's lives, and they hear the stories that are told. When someone is hurting, they know about it, and they minister to them. These people are the eyes and ears.

What a shame it would be if a person who serves in some humble but important place said, "Because I'm not as noticed as the eye, I'm not of the body." Paul pointed out that we are unavoidably and unalterably part of the body. Both the plodding, humble foot and the listening ear are parts of the body.

In verse 18, Paul suggested that all members of the body are important and that God has put together the body in a way that pleases Him. Think about that.

Many years ago my wife and I started a church in Northern California. On our first Sunday, eight people came. We have also served much larger churches. In every church we served, regardless of the size, God has always provided the people needed to accomplish what He intended for that church to accomplish. If the church needed construction work, then God sent construction workers. If the church needed teachers and leaders, God sent people to help the church in those areas. God has always supplied the church according to His will and His purpose for that church. God has gifted the body as it pleased Him.

We are one body even though we are different. We are one body even though we are many. We are one body regardless of our social or economic setting. We are one body regardless of our place in the body. We are one body, and that body is pleasing to God.

Even when the leaders of the church understand that fellowship is more than cookies and punch, getting the congregation to think of fellowship in its broader meaning may be difficult. Here are some steps you as a leader might take to enhance fellowship in your church. Consider specific ways you might apply each step in your congregation. Think of persons who will join you in making fellowship a strong function of your church.

Model Fellowship

As a leader in a smaller membership church, you should be in fellowship with everyone in the body. Of course, you may have some special friends within your congregation. Everyone needs friends—including the pastor and other church leaders. Bur your close friendships should not keep you from having fellowship with all the people in the church—both members and those the church is trying to reach.

All church members need the fellowship of their pastor and other leaders in the congregation, and in a smaller membership church these relationships are even more important. Model strong, healthy fellowship in your church by being involved in fellowship with all the people in your congregation.

To accomplish this you may have to enlist the help of others to know who needs someone to get under the burden with them at that moment. My wife always helped me to understand when someone needed a special word of encouragement or a special kind of ministry. Together we were able to model fellowship as she exercised her gift of discernment and helped me understand who was in need of fellowship. Find someone to partner with you in this ministry.

Another way to model fellowship before the congregation God has called you to lead is to be in fellowship even with those who might in some ways be in conflict with you. I remember a few years ago I preached a sermon that made one of my church members angry with me. He came to me after the service. I could tell he was angry, and in his anger he said some things to me that were somewhat unkind. I tried to maintain a close and open relationship with him and tried to keep the doors of fellowship open. I didn't respond in anger against him.

A few weeks later my friend became ill. In his time of need, I went to him and got under the load with him. I prayed with him and cried with him. We struggled together about the illness that had suddenly come to him. I had fellowship with that man. Soon it was obvious that even though we were different kinds of men, even though we had different views about the subject of my sermon and probably several other things, we had something in common that was much more significant than anything that divided us.

Because I had strong fellowship with him, that fellowship was an overriding factor. It overcame the conflict that could have arisen from our differences. Fellowship with those who disagree with you. Fellowship with those what attack you. Fellowship with those who are angry with you. In doing so you can model what it means to be a church that is healthy, carrying out the fellowship function of the church.

Brag on Fellowship

A few weeks ago my pastor asked me to go to the funeral home and minister to a family that had lost a loved one. When I arrived at the funeral home, I noticed that several church members were already there. Those church members were fellowshipping with their sister in Christ. The woman who had lost her mother needed someone to get under the load with her. I performed the funeral service, said the prayers, read the Scripture, and ministered to her in the way a pastor can; but she needed a sister in Christ to sit down with her, put her arm around her, say, "I love you," and cry with her. That's fellowship.

When I got back to the church, I bragged on those church members, and I told the pastor about their ministry; and the pastor bragged on those church members to the congregation. Because we were bragging on those people who did a good job at fellowship, we were encouraging other church members to do the same thing.

Find people doing something good and tell the story. You can be sure the devil will tell the story when something bad happens, so make it your responsibility to tell everyone when something good happens. If you see your people having fellowship with one another (remember fellowship is more than cookies and punch), if you see your people getting under the load with a brother or sister in Christ, tell that story in an appropriate way. You may need to get permission from the ones who are participating in that fellowship time, but let others know about so it can be an encouragement to them.

Brag on your people in a healthy, scriptural way. Not only will the one who has been fellowshipping and is receiving praise for it be encouraged, but other people will be encouraged to do the same thing. Brag on fellowship when you see it taking place in your church.

Plan for Fellowship

Be intentional about the fellowship function of the church. To be sure, you'll want to schedule some old-fashioned fellowships. Even the cookies-and-punch kind are good at this point—not as good as the homemade ice cream kind, but good. Fellowship does include those kinds of gatherings. It's good for a church to get together after church on Sunday night or for a fellowship event one night during the week. That's helpful. Plan those events. Put them on the church calendar, and make sure they happen. Plan for fellowship in other ways, too.

Times of grief in the church family are times when God's people need someone to get under the load with them, to fellowship with them. Organize your church in such a way that your people are aware of opportunities when fellowship is needed.

You'll notice that there is a strong connection between fellowship and ministry. In fact, fellowship is a ministry many times in the church. Provide opportunities for people in your congregation to hold up one another and to be involved in fellowship with one another.

When church members face a crisis and you know they need a brother or sister to walk with them, why not make a phone call to those you know who might have some experience in that area. Ask them to fellowship with their brother or sister. Then extend this type fellowship ministry to those in your community that the church is trying to reach. Plan for fellowship in the church.

Encourage Sunday School classes to spend time in fellowship. One of the most healthy classes in the church I attend gathers for a time of fellowship a few minutes before Sunday School on the first Sunday of the month. Another class goes out to eat together once a quarter. The key is to spend time in fellowship with one another.

Build Fellowship in Worship

One of the reasons God instructed the church not to forsake assembling together is that we need to fellowship with one another as a part of our worship experience (see Heb. 10:25). One of my favorite times during the worship service is when the pianist plays a hymn and the pastor encourages all the members, as brothers and sisters in Christ, to spend a few minutes in fellowship with one another. What a joy it is to share a smile, a handshake or hug, and a warm greeting with others in the worship service. Children enjoy it, too. This simple act makes worship a warm and enjoyable fellowship time.

When we read God's Word.—We also fellowship together around the Word of God during worship services. As the pastor preaches, we have something in common. We are all hearing and seeing the Word of God and understanding it together. The blinders are pulled back from our eyes as the Lord's Holy Spirit helps us to understand the Word.

As the pastor expounds God's Word to us, we share fellowship in the Word of God. Let's make the most of this fellowship time. The church can fellowship together in worship when the pastor announces the Scripture passage for the day. When we hear those pages turning and see the people sitting around us holding open Bibles in their hands, that's fellowship. We are sharing something important in common, and that important thing is the Word of God. Let's fellowship around the Word of God.

When we sing.—The same thing can be said for the hymns. When we stand together to sing the great hymns of the faith, we share fellowship as we focus our thoughts and our attention on the message of that hymn. Whether we're singing a Bible-based hymn or a new praise that directs our thoughts to the Lord Himself, we are one body addressing our praise or our concerns to God. Fellowship around the hymns we sing.

When we pray.—We also should fellowship around the prayers we pray in times of worship. Praying when we are gathered together in public worship is different from praying at home, isn't it? We call it "corporate prayer" because we are praying a prayer that expresses the needs of an entire body of Christ. Let's fellowship together around those prayer times. Encourage your people to join with the one who is praying aloud.

As one voices the prayer, the rest of the people are united in thought, in prayer, and in spirit around the expressed prayer of the one who is leading. The congregation experiences a time of fellowship as they join together in expressing their heart's desires, sincere thanks, or expressions of praise to the Lord.

When we celebrate baptism and the Lord's Supper.—The ordinances also offer precious times of fellowship in the worship experience. Baptism is a wonderful time of fellowship because all members of our churches have been baptized, and we join together in fellowship when we ask a new believer or a new member of our church to join with us by being baptized into our fellowship. We have something in common. We are one body. That baptism is a testimony to the death, burial, and resurrection of Christ. It's a picture of the end of our old life and the beginning of our new life in Christ. It's a picture of our sins being washed away. It's a picture of renewal as we rise up out of the waters of the baptistry. We share a strong sense of fellowship around the fact that all of us have been baptized into the body of Christ.

The Lord's Supper is also a time of fellowship. In 1 Corinthians 11:18, Paul spoke of the Lord's Supper observance. He said, "For first of all, when ye come together in the church, I hear that there be divisions among you." Paul was pointing out the importance of putting aside divisions when we come to fellowship together at the Lord's table.

People from different economic and social backgrounds came together in the Corinthian church. Some brought a feast and spread it out; others where poor and could only bring a little morsel of bread. Paul said that when you come together in that way, "this is not to eat the Lord's upper" (v. 22). He suggested that in coming to the Lord's Supper we come for different reasons than just to fill our bellies. Certainly we know that's true. The tiny portions of bread and juice we commonly use today are reminders that the Lord's Supper is not about physical hunger but about fellowship. It's about reminding us that we, as the body of Christ, have something wonderful, powerful, and compelling in common. We have in common that Jesus Christ, the Son of God, allowed His body to be broken for us. We have in common that Jesus shed His blood for the remission of our sins.

The Lord's Supper is a time to put aside anything that might divide us. You, as a leader in your congregation, should remind your people of the fellowship aspects of the Lord's Supper. If you are the pastor of your church, you certainly should remind them as you begin the observance that the Lord's Supper is a time for unity. It's a time to put aside any division that might exist in the body because that which we have in common is more significant than anything which might divide us. We have in common nothing less than the broken body and the shed blood of Jesus. As we remember what Jesus has done for us, we are reminded of our strong fellowship in the body of Christ.

In verse 26, Paul said, "For as often as ye eat this bread, and drink this cup, ye do shew the Lord's death till he come." The observance of the Lord's Supper shows anyone who might observe it that Jesus died for our sins. His body was broken; His blood was shed for the remission of our sins. But the observance of the Lord's Supper also shows that we, as the body of Christ, have in common a belief that Jesus is coming back. The return of Christ as our focus is a fellowship point in the observance of Lord's Supper.

Build Fellowship by Participating in Ministry and Missions

A few years ago I was pastor of the Spring Creek Baptist Church near Kentwood, Louisiana. The fine people of that church decided to go on a mission trip to a small town in Nevada. In the daytime we worked on their building and conducted a Vacation Bible School. At night we led worship services. We knocked on every door in that small community telling people about Jesus.

Some interesting things happened. Yes, we did a lot of ministry. We accomplished a lot in the lives of the pastor and the members of that church and some of the lost people who came to know the Lord during that week. But something else happened. We built a strong bond of fellowship among those who went on the mission trip. Strong fellowship takes place as God's people work together side by side, involving themselves in ministry or missions.

The men who replaced the roof that week had something in common that was strong and powerful. They had worked hard together in the hot

Nevada sun. That was a strong fellowship point for them.

Those who conducted the Vacation Bible School had stories to tell about children who heard the gospel for the first time and the appreciation of the few workers from that small church who were helped by their coworkers from Louisiana in conducting that VBS. When they went back home, they shared a strong bond of love and fellowship that existed because they had labored together, side by side in ministry, in missions, and even in physical labor as they carried out the Great Commission. We build fellowship in times of ministry and missions.

Building fellowship in missions and ministry doesn't have to involve a trip across the country. You might just involve the people of your church in a local missions enterprise, or you might build fellowship in your church just by having a workday. I remember times when I have worked with the other men of the congregation to repair the roof, to put up a steeple, to mow the grass, or to clean up debris. Those are strong times of fellowship, and fellowship is built in your congregation as you labor together side by side. Build fellowship by involving your people in ministry.

Build Fellowship by Repairing Breaks in the Fellowship

Churches experience five levels of conflict.

1. Conflict begins as a problem to be solved. It's simple. There really isn't a conflict yet, just a problem to be solved.

2. Conflict escalates to a disagreement. At this point the conflict is a little bit more serious. It's gone beyond just a problem to be solved. Now people have different ideas about what should be done, and a disagreement exists. At this level conflict is relatively easy to resolve because it is nothing more than a disagreement.

3. If conflict continues to build, it will become a contest. At this point the object for those involved in the conflict is to win the contest. At this point conflict has little to do with the original cause of the conflict. Winning is the most significant factor.

4. Conflict then escalates to the stage called fight or flight. At this level of conflict, some people say, "This is my church, and nothing is going to run me off." These people have decided to stay and fight. Other folks involved in the conflict might approach it by saying: "I just can't

worship in a place where such conflict exists. I'm going to find another church." These people have decided to flee. It's fight or flight. Either way great damage is done to the church. Level 4 conflict is rarely resolved. The better goal is to manage conflict at this point.

5. The highest level of conflict is an intractable situation. This is the conflict which has escalated to the point that folks in the church literally will not speak to one another.

As you can see in looking at these levels of conflict, fellowship can be broken, even destroyed, by conflict in the church. As a leader in the church, you are responsible for monitoring disagreements in the church. Do everything you can to repair the breaks in the fellowship before they escalate beyond a problem to be solved or a disagreement in the body. When your conflict is a problem or a disagreement, you can resolve it. You can help in that situation, and the best way to keep it from escalating is to intervene early to bring conflicting parties together. Encourage them to work toward a win-win solution. Remind them that they are one body even though they are different. Build fellowship by repairing the breaks in the fellowship.

Build Fellowship by Remembering the Single-Cell Principle

Small churches have a tendency to think of themselves as one cell or one unit. That is, most smaller membership churches do everything together. If there is a fellowship of any kind, it will likely include everyone in the church. Most smaller membership churches do not plan fellowship activities just for young adults or just for senior adults. The exception is probably the youth ministry or children's ministry. They probably provide some things exclusively for them. But among the adults there usually is just one group, and the people in the church think of themselves as a part of that one group.

Build fellowship in your church by encouraging your people to gather for fellowship in smaller groups. For example, encourage a Young Adult Sunday School class to begin the practice of gathering monthly or quarterly for fellowship. Perhaps on Saturday night they'd like to go to dinner together. Encourage the senior adults to come together for fellowship in some ways that would meet their needs that perhaps younger adults wouldn't enjoy. Encourage them to gather as a group and to build fellowship in that way. The more you can encourage your people to provide fellowship opportunities in smaller groups, the stronger your church will be. And while you are building fellowship, you are also building some strong relationship groups that will be inviting to prospects and to potential members. Build fellowship by providing fellowship opportunities for smaller groups in the church.

Chapter 11

MINISTRY

In Mark 10:45, Jesus said, "For even the Son of man came not to be ministered unto, but to minister, and to give his life a ransom for many." When I read that verse, the word "*even*" really jumps out at me. Jesus taught His followers an important lesson when He said, "*even* the Son of man . . . came to minister." The strong implication is that if Jesus, the King of kings, came to minister, surely, certainly, all of us ought to be involved in ministry.

In Ephesians 5:25-27, Paul said: "Husbands, love your wives, even as Christ also loved the church, and gave himself for it; that he might sanctify and cleanse it with the washing of water by the word, that he might present it to himself a glorious church, not having spot, or wrinkle, or any such thing; but that it should be holy and without blemish." In that passage the Bible teaches us that Jesus loved the church. If you're involved in the church, you're involved in a ministry which is loved by Jesus. Not only did Jesus love the church, but Jesus gave Himself for the church. The word "*sanctify*," in verse 26 means "set apart for special service." In the Old Testament we find an illustration of what it means to be sanctified.

In Exodus 40, the Bible records God's instructions concerning the tabernacle in the wilderness. Moses received these instructions from God Himself. The instructions were that the tabernacle would be built a certain way. When everything was prepared, Moses was instructed to move the altar into place, and then Moses said the altar was to be sanctified. He was to put the laver in place. The laver was a place of ceremonial cleansing. It contained water that was used in symbolic and ceremonial cleansing of the priest's hands before he entered into the tabernacle to serve. When the laver was put in place, God said, "Sanctify the laver."

Now think about that for a moment. When God said, "Sanctify the altar," He was saying that this altar was no ordinary raised platform. It was to be special. It was to be different from all the other raised platforms one might see. This altar was a place where sacrifice would be made to God. It was sanctified because it was special; it was set apart for service.

When the laver was put into place as God instructed, the laver was sanctified. That meant that the laver was to be used in a different way. It was not just a bowl on a pedestal. It was to be used in a way that was distinctive and unique in all the world because the laver would be for the ceremonial cleansing of the priests as they entered into the tabernacle to lead the people in worship. When these pieces of furniture in the tabernacle were sanctified, they were set apart for special service. They were unique and never would be viewed the same way again.

Exodus 40 continues to say that Aaron, the high priest, and his sons were to enter the tabernacle; and then Aaron and his sons were to be sanctified. When Aaron and his sons were sanctified, they were set apart for a special service. No longer were they the same men as before. No longer would they be pursuing the same kinds of occupation as before. Now they were set apart for special service.

In Ephesians 5, Paul said that Jesus loved and sanctified the church. Christ is still in the process of sanctifying the church. We, as God's people, are set apart for special service. The church is not a building. The church is not wood and mortar, stone and metal. The church is people; and when people are set apart for special service, they will never be the same again.

Ephesians 5:26-27 teaches that God's people are set apart for special ministry. Jesus said, "By this shall all men know that ye are my disciples, if ye have love one to another" (John 14:35). A church that is not a ministering church is not fulfilling the commands or the expectations of Jesus. Jesus loved the church and gave Himself for it in order that it might be set apart for special service for ministry. Our churches ought to be ministering churches. Ministry is one of the five functions every church must do in order to be a healthy, balanced church.

If you went into almost any small church this coming Sunday morning and asked, "Is this a loving, caring church?" the response would be almost universal. Every smaller church considers itself to be a place where people love one another. Unfortunately, what that often means is that we love those like us. We love those who are already in the family. But if you want us to love and minister to those who are outside our family or those who are different from us, you might get a different response. A real loving church, a real ministering church is one where people love one another. Yes, they love those in the family, but they also are willing to love and minister to those outside the family. Sometimes leading a smaller membership church to be focused and active in ministry can be a challenge. Here are a few tips to help you along the way.

Love People

To lead the smaller membership church to be a ministering church, you must model ministry, and that begins with loving people. I have some friends who are pastors of smaller churches for whom loving people is just a natural, normal thing. They are highly relational, and it is easy for them to be with people and to love people. I have some other friends who are pastors of smaller membership churches who say, "Pastoring a smaller membership church would be easy if it weren't for the people."

Of course, the church is people; and all of us must love people if we're going to be actively involved in a healthy church. But for some pastors, loving people is not as easy as it is for others. Maybe it's that they love people down deep inside but have difficulty relating to people in a healthy manner. It is absolutely essential, however, that every pastor lead his church by modeling a love for people.

If you're not highly relational, if showing your love for others is more of a challenge for you, let me suggest that you ask God to give you a genuine love for the people with whom you serve. When a pastor loves his people, it is much more likely that they will love him in return. When you stand before your people on Sunday morning, God has laid a message on your heart, you're ready to deliver that message to the people of the Lord. Look at those people. Don't see them just as a crowd. Don't even see them just as a congregation. Instead, look at those people and see individuals for whom Jesus died. Think of the hurts those people have endured. Think of the hardships they've carried through the years, and think of the family trials and difficulties they may face. Think of the places they work and how they stand for Jesus day by day. Think of what they might have experienced in their childhoods. Get to know them as individual people.

When you look out at that sea of faces, don't see just a crowd or a congregation; see those individuals. Think about the gifts God has given them. See the worth in each one of those people in your congregation. On one side sits a person who may not be good at meeting people and making friends but has a good, clear mind.

On the other side you may see a person who is so relational, loving, and ,caring that he or she doesn't care much at all about details. Loving people is the top concern.

Both of those folks have worth in the kingdom of God. Consider them and consider the values the strengths that each brings to the kingdom of God and to your church. This little exercise will help you love people and show your love for them.

Another exercise you might do to help you show your love for the people is, on a weekly basis, to show your love for someone in the congregation in a tangible way. Perhaps the Lord will lead you to say a simple thank you to someone in the congregation who serves faithfully. Maybe you will feel led to express thanks to someone whose work is not often noticed or who is seldom recognized. Perhaps the way you could show your love is just by saying how much you appreciate what they do. Or you may feel drawn to someone who is one of your best friends or to someone who has even been an antagonist in the church. Regardless of who it is, discover the worth in those persons and tell them how much you appreciate what they do in the kingdom of God and in your church.

Another way to show your love for the people with whom God has called you to serve is to recognize some members from the pulpit. Most smaller churches would benefit from hearing their pastors bragging on them every week. One to three minutes is enough to tell a few persons in the congregation how you appreciate them.

Another way to show your love for someone in the church or to model loving others before your church is to minister to someone who is in need. Perhaps a lonely person in your church needs a visit from the pastor. Maybe someone you know is facing a difficulty, and you just know that your spending a few minutes with them would be greatly appreciated, even a phone call and a prayer uttered over the phone lines. Lead your congregation to be a church that is healthy in ministry by loving people yourself. You, as a leader in the church, model loving others.

Know People

Lead your church to be a ministering church by getting to know the people with whom God has called you to serve. You know their names, and you know the family relationships, but have you really invested yourself enough in these people to get to know them? I hope the answer is yes, but it is possible to serve people, to preach to them, to lead them and never really get to know them.

The best way to get to know people is to spend time with them. One of the real joys of a smaller membership church is that members have the opportunity to know one another. Perhaps it would be a good idea for many pastors of smaller membership churches to develop a schedule by which they will visit the people in the congregation. This time need not take away from visiting prospects for your church or those who need ministry, but it's a good idea just to visit everyone in your church. Do the people who come after week, who attend every Sunday morning and Sunday night and Wednesday night ever get a visit? Just drop by to see them in their home environment and pray with them in their home. Let them know that you care about them. It's a good idea for those people to know that you have an interest in them. Get to know them personally.

When you visit in someone's home, ask questions about that person's family. Look at the pictures on the walls. Those pictures represent some of the people who are most precious to that family. Ask, "Is this your daughter?" Or: "Are these your parents? Are these your grandchildren?" Let them know that you are interested in hearing the story that goes along with that picture. Joy comes to people's faces when they talk to their pastor about beloved family members. Maybe they need to tell you about the husband or wife that passed away a few years ago. Maybe they need to tell you about their son or daughter who graduated from college and how proud they are that that member of their family has achieved such wonderful status. Get to know folks by visiting in their homes.

Another way to get to know people is by really listening when you talk to them or they talk to you at the church. For some pastors, maybe even most pastors, there's a natural tendency to rush from one person to the next on Sunday morning and not really take the time to invest yourself in hearing what the person is saying. If you're like most pastors, you have a couple of people in your church who come to you every Sunday morning to tell you about their aches and pains. You get tired of listening to them, don't you?

Take the time. Really listen to what they have to say. Look in their eyes. Call their names during the conversation. Ask a question that indicates your interest and requests further information. Lead your people to minister by getting to know them.

Loving people and knowing people are actions you, as a leader, must take to model ministry before your congregation. If you're involved in ministry, your people are more likely to be involved in ministry. And, of course, your church will be healthy in doing the ministry function of the church.

Motivate People

After you model ministry before your church, it is time to motivate the people of your church to be involved in ministry themselves. The first step in motivating your people to minister is to teach them what the Word of God says about ministry. Open your Bible to Mark 10, and teach them that Jesus Himself came as a minister. Since even Jesus was a minister, certainly they ought to minister to others. Teach them about Jesus' washing the disciples feet, and suggest that they should be servants to those around them. Teach them what the Bible says about feeding the hungry and clothing the needy. Teach them what Ephesians says about the church as a sanctified body. Teach them that the word *sanctified* means "set apart for a special service or set apart for special ministry." If your people know that the Bible teaches that they ought to be involved in ministry, many of them will choose to be involved in ministry.

Don't become discouraged too easily or too quickly in teaching your people about ministry. Many churches have a few crusty, calloused members who will not be motivated to minister just because the Bible tells them they should. But some folks in your church will be motivated to minister when they see the clear teaching of the Scripture on this subject.

Preach about ministry.—Once in a while you ought to preach a sermon on Sunday morning about ministry, but Sunday night and Wednesday nights are excellent times for motivational Bible study on ministry. Target your message toward the more mature or at least the most faithful in attendance in your congregation. Teach them what the Bible says with the clear expectation and understanding that they will certainly accept the teaching of Scripture and minister. By the way, when you teach your people that the Bible says churches ought to be involved in ministry, teach them to define that ministry as going beyond those who are part of the family already, going beyond those who are like us. Teach them to minister outside the four walls of the church because the church that ministers there will be effective in reaching people outside the church.

Provide ministry models.—Another way to motivate your people to minister is to provide some ministry heroes among your people. In our Baptist family we have some wonderful missionaries who have literally given their lives in ministry to others. Frequently, we should tell their stories from the pulpit. For information on current heroes, check the International Mission Board's web site from time to time.

In addition to telling the stories of our missionary heroes on Sunday morning or Sunday night, once a year most smaller churches ought to find some way to have a missionary visit and speak in your services. Not only will this build motivation for your people to be involved in ministry by showing them a real live ministry hero, but it also will provide a certain continuity and support for Cooperative Program giving and giving to missions offerings. Every church benefits from seeing and hearing the missionaries they support. Some of the leaders of your missions organizations will likely be happy to help you bring those missionaries into your church.

You may also have in your community a retired pastor or denominational worker such as a director of missions who is a ministry hero. If you know someone like that, why not honor that person? That would motivate your people. Maybe you could set aside a Sunday as Ministry Hero Day. Brag on the person. Tell his or her story. Consider presenting some kind of a gift and have a fellowship after church. Let your people know that ministry is something special and important in the family of God.

Provide ministry opportunities.—Another way to motivate people to do ministry is to provide ministry opportunities that make it convenient for people to be involved. There probably are people in your congregation who have a heart for ministry and would like to be involved in ministry, but they consider themselves incapable of doing ministry. Maybe they think of ministry as something reserved for preachers. Maybe they think that to minister they must give their lives to become missionaries. They need to learn and understand from you as their leader that ministry opportunities come to everyone and there are all kinds of ministry opportunities.

A few years ago I was serving as pastor of a smaller church in North Alabama. The deacons got together one Saturday morning and went to the home of one of the widows in our congregation to winterize her home. It took us a couple of hours. Some of the fellows put plastic on the windows to keep out the cold. Others put up some insulation and used a little bit of caulk here and there and wrapped some the pipes so they wouldn't freeze. Real ministry, real caring ministry involves all kinds of people with all kinds of skills.

We need ministry opportunities that are presented at all times of the week and at all times of the day so that people who work different shifts or have different days off have opportunities to be involved in ministry. Ministry can be as varied as winterizing a home or visiting someone who is lonely or sick. Ministry could include visiting the jail or prison in your community, or it could include providing some food or clothing for those in need. One person might be involved in ministry by serving as a greeter in your church on Sunday morning, welcoming folks with a big smile and a friendly handshake. Another person might make regular visits to homebound members of the church and community. How varied and are the ministry opportunities in your church and in your community? Motivate your people to be involved in ministry by providing lots of times and places and ways in which they can be participate.

Organize People for Ministry

Most Baptist churches have in place the organizational structure to provide excellence in ministry. In fact, the Sunday School organization that already exists in your church is one of the best organizations that could be created to involve the people of your church in ministry.

If your Sunday School is like most smaller membership Sunday Schools, it has a pretty good teaching ministry. Some teachers in your Sunday School have probably been involved in teaching the Bible for many years. Around those good teachers are loyal class members who love that teacher and enjoy that Sunday School class. Those people get together every week, and they do a good job of studying the Word of God. They may not do quite as well at ministry. They take care of one another, but if ministry means caring for those outside that class, then they probably need to improve a little bit. Every church needs two things to make ministry through the Sunday School more effective.

First, every church should consider its enrollment as a ministry list.—Does a person have to prove his or her worth in order to become a member of your Sunday School? I hope your church is not one of those places where a person must come three Sundays in a row to prove their worth before being allowed to become a member of your Sunday School.

Think of your Sunday School enrollment as people who need ministry. If you suggested to your Sunday School teachers this coming Sunday that they begin to think of their class members as a ministry list, some of your teachers would resist that. Do you know why they don't want to think of their Sunday School enrollment as a ministry list? They don't want to think of their Sunday School members as people who need ministry. And some of your teachers don't have the time or the inclination to involve themselves in ministry. They don't mind teaching, but they don't want to involve themselves in people's lives because that requires giving their most precious possession, their time.

As a leader of a smaller membership church, you need to set the pace for others by presenting them the idea that the Sunday School enrollment ought to be thought of as a list of people who need ministry. In fact, when you drop people from your Sunday School roll simply because they have not attended regularly, you are probably eliminating their last chance for salvation and their last chance for someone to minister to them. When you drop someone from the Sunday School roll, perhaps no one from your church will pray for them, no one will contact them, and no one will minister to them. Keep those people on the Sunday School roll.

In order for this concept of Sunday School enrollment as a ministry list to be effective, eliminate all the incentives to drop people from the Sunday School rolls. If you recognize the class with 100 percent of its enrollment present, you're providing a strong incentive to drop people from the roll. After all, the easiest way to get 100 percent of your class in attendance is to drop those who don't attend regularly.

There are some legitimate reasons for dropping people from the Sunday School rolls—when they move out of the community, when they request to be dropped, and when they become active and join another congregation. But until one of those things happens, keep those people on your Sunday School roll and think of them as a ministry list.

Organize your Sunday School to minister to the people on that ministry list.—The best way to do that is through care group leaders. Lots of smaller church pastors have read or heard about care groups and have decided that the care group system is too complex to work in the smaller membership church. That is not true. Care group leaders have three essential duties. When you limit the duties of care group leaders to these three tasks that, you can more easily enlist people to be care group leaders. The care group ministry can be an effective organizational tool to mobilize your Sunday School to minister to Sunday School members and prospects.

1. *Care group leaders should contact the people in their group each week.*—In order for people to make those contacts every week, they have to keep care groups small. Care group leaders should be responsible for a group no larger than five people. Anyone can find time to call five

friends, to see them in church, or to see them at the market or at school every week.

Of course, if care leaders call the people in their care group and say, "Where were you last week, you sorry rascal?" they will not want to receive that call every week. If, on the other hand, the care leader calls people and focuses on prayer and relationships, people will welcome that ministry call every week. Train your care group leaders to call the people in their group every week to say: "I'm just calling to see how you're doing and to see if you have prayer concern you'd like me to take back to the class this coming week. Tell me how your week has been."

If care leaders call people weekly with a loving interest in them, with a focus on prayer and getting prayer requests from them, they'll find that they can call those people every week until the Lord comes back and no one will get angry at them. They will welcome the call.

2. *Care group leaders should pray every week for the people in their group.*—Many Sunday School members who are potential care group leaders are already involved in prayer and would be delighted to pray for five people by name every week.

3. *Care group leaders should minister to the people in their care group or refer them to someone else who can minister to them.*—When a care group leader calls a member of the group and discovers a ministry need which the group can meet, then that care group leader should directly perform the ministry or enlist the group's help. If, however, the care group leader discovers some ministry need and the care leader feels incapable of ministering in that situation, he or she should refer that need to someone else. Let the Sunday School teacher know. Let the Sunday School director know. Let one of the deacons know, or let the pastor know. By simply making a phone call, the care leader can refer ministry needs to others. Every care group leader should either minister to the needs discovered or refer to someone else who can minister.

These three duties are all a care group leader really needs to do. It is possible to enlist some folks in your church to contact, pray, and either minister or refer. Let me suggest an approach by which you can do this.

Set a date for care group leader training.—Perhaps a good time for your church is lunch after church on Sunday morning. Invite your people to bring a potluck lunch and train them as care group leaders. Perhaps your leaders would like to do that one weeknight. You need only about an hour of their time for the training.

Encourage your Sunday School teachers to begin enlisting care group leaders.—With the training date in mind, ask each Sunday School teacher to attempt to enlist one care group leader for every five members of the Sunday School class. Remember, they are only enlisting them to come to the training. The people who are enlisted are not even agreeing to serve as care group leaders; they're only agreeing to come to the training.

Some teachers will enlist all of their care group leaders. Others will need help from you as a pastor or from the Sunday School director or from another leader in the church.

At the training cover the three duties of care leaders.

1. Contact every member of your care group every week.
2. Pray for every member of your care group every week.
3. Minister or refer when ministry needs are encountered.

Spend the bulk of your time talking about that weekly phone call. Try to minimize the possibility that someone will call with a caustic or negative approach. If they call people every week and berate them about their poor attendance, they will not welcome those calls; but if they call people every week and focus on praying for them and others in the class, caring about them, and discovering ministry needs, the people in your congregation will welcome those calls from their care group leaders.

Another important way to organize your church for ministry is through your deacon body.—Whether your deacons do significant administrative work in your church, your deacons can be involved in ministry. The deacon family ministry plan is a popular and effective approach for involving deacons in ministry. Spend time every month in deacons meeting talking about ministry opportunities. In some smaller membership churches the best approach is to spend a few minutes talking about the needs that have been discovered in the community. Offer your deacons opportunities to be involved in ministry.

If, for example, you talk about the needs of your congregation as a part of your prayer time in deacons meeting, you might discover that someone in the church needs a visit from someone. The pastor could say: "I certainly am going to visit that person, but I wonder if one of you might have some time this week to drop by. I think two visits would really mean a lot to this person."

Perhaps summer is coming, the grass is growing, and everyone is cranking up the lawn mowers. In the deacons meeting one of the men might share a senior adult's need to have the yard cut. A deacons meeting is a good time to discuss how the church could meet that need. One of the deacons might be able to take time to mow the yard of that senior adult. Or if that's not a possibility, the deacons might be able to find someone to volunteer, or the church could hire someone to cut the grass all summer. Perhaps the youth in the church could be mobilized to meet the need.

This is deacon ministry, and deacons ought to be involved. Take time in deacons meetings to discuss ministry. Most deacon bodies would appreciate the opportunity to be involved in ministry. It will be good for them and good for the church as well. Organize your deacon body for effective ministry in the congregation.

Individual Ministries

Organizing your Sunday School and your deacon body for ministry is important, but it is probably not enough to have a complete approach to ministry in your church. Some people in your congregation ought to be involved in ministry, yet they are not deacons and would not serve as a care group leader. Find ways to offer individuals in your church opportunities for ministry.

When ministry needs are discovered, a word spoken from the pulpit or a personal word to an individual who should be involved in ministry can provide a link between the person and the ministry that needs to be accomplished. Invest your time and energy as a leader in discovering needs and linking individuals who are capable of meeting those needs. Many people in your church will appreciate the opportunity to meet needs by ministering. They will appreciate the confidence you have in them as a leader in that church when you come to them to say: "I know of a need. Perhaps you could serve the Lord by ministering in this way."

Some ministry needs, however, are beyond the scope of your local community. Mission trips to other parts of the nation or even other parts of the world can present significant ministry opportunities. Recently a friend of mine spoke with excitement of the plans in his church to take a mission trip across the country to build a church house for a small congregation in a faraway state. Several churches in a community have a big steak dinner in the spring of the year to raise money to build a church building or to do another type of construction project. Many state conventions have an office that coordinates such ministry activities. Perhaps individuals in your congregation would enjoy participating in one of those construction trips or some other kind of missionary or ministry trip.

Another friend recently told me of a mission trip to a country that was a part of the former Soviet Union. My friend and several others labored to remodel a house and make it into a church building. It was the kind of project that could be completed in the amount of time they had set aside. Everyone was enriched by the experience. Give your people ministry opportunities by providing information to participate in mission trips across the world. What a blessing it would be to smaller membership churches if one or two people in those churches participated in some missionary trip that carried them to a foreign country and allowed them to meet International Mission Board missionaries and allowed them to see the needs of the people of that land. What a blessing it would be when they came back and told their stories to their congregation. Involve your church in ministry by giving individuals many opportunities to participate in ministry.

Chapter 12

WORSHIP

Recently I was invited to preach in a church in the Nashville, Tennessee, area. The church was rather formal in its approach to worship. The deacons and I lined up in the hallway and marched in as the service began. When we entered, everyone became quiet. They remained quiet and outwardly unresponsive for the rest of the worship service. The traditional service was conducted with dignity and (frankly) predictability.

The next Sunday I preached in another nearby church. It was completely different from the week before. When I entered the worship center, everyone was talking and enjoying fellowship with one another. This spirit of openness and responsiveness continued throughout the service.

To tell the truth, I enjoyed the second service more. But I learned something from preaching at these two different churches. Real, genuine worship happened in both places. Regardless of our personal preferences, worship is not limited to one style or approach.

Lessons on Worship

Worship is entering the presence of God.—In Hebrews 10:19-25 the author of Hebrews provides an important lesson about worship. Verse 19 says we have boldness to enter the presence of God. What a thought! We have been given the high privilege of boldly entering the presence of God Himself.

The picture that's drawn in verses 19-21 is of the Old Testament tabernacle or temple. It was surrounded by courts where only certain ones were allowed to enter. In that temple was a holy place curtained off by a thick veil. Inside that was a holy of holies that was even more sacred. There the high priest was allowed to enter only once a year on the day of atonement after sacrifices had been offered for himself and for the sins of his family and for the sins of his nation.

The holy of holies was a sacred place that represented to the Hebrew people the presence of God Himself. When the author of Hebrews said that we have been allowed to enter boldly into the holiest, he meant that we as God's people have been invited to walk boldly through that veil into the presence of the Holy God.

Worship is drawing near to God.—About once a month a young man comes to our home and goes into every room in our house. The young man's name is Brian, and he calls the day before to make sure we're going to be home. Brian comes to our home and sprays our house for bugs. He's the pest control guy.

A few times my pastor has come into my home. He came by when my wife's mother died. He came to pray with us, to share with us, to comfort us from the Scriptures. When Brother Don came into our home, he did more than just enter into our presence. He drew near to us because of the special relationship we have with him. There was more to his visit than just physically entering into our home.

The difference in the pastor's visits to my home reminds me of the lesson in Hebrews 10:22. Yes, you may enter the presence of God, but you're invited by God to do something more. You're invited to draw near to Him. You're invited into a relationship of closeness and intimacy. Worship is more than just coming into the presence of God; worship is drawing near to God.

Worship is holding on to your profession of faith.—Hebrews 10:23 does not say that we're to hold on to our salvation. That's God's work. God is holding on to our salvation. That is secure. The Bible says that we ought to hold to a profession of our faith.

When I come to the Lord's house to worship, when I gather with God's people to worship, I am professing my faith in Christ. I choose to come to a place on Sunday morning where I know the name of Jesus will be lifted up. That's a profession of my faith. I choose to come to a place where I know that the songs of Zion are going to be ringing through the air, and I choose to profess my faith by singing and participating in those songs. I choose to come to a place where I know that the Word of God will be read and studied; and when I come to that place of worship, I am holding up the profession of my faith so that anyone who might hear or see me knows that I belong to Jesus. I love to study His Word. Worship is holding to the profession of our faith.

It's interesting to think about Sunday nights in this regard. I can choose to do a lot of things on Sunday night. I can choose to stay at home and watch television. I can choose to go to some other place, but my family and I choose to go to the Lord's house on Sunday night. Why? Partly because it's a profession of our faith. We enjoy being with the people of God, and we benefit from the Bible study, but we also participate in that Sunday night worship experience because it's a way of saying to my neighbors and to my community and to my children, even to myself, that I belong to Jesus. I want to hold up the profession of my faith. Worship is holding on to the profession of your faith.

Worship is considering one another.—Hebrews 10:24 reminds us that worship is considering one another. That verse says that we should provoke one another to love and to good works. Baptists are pretty good at provoking one another, but this verse says that we should provoke in good ways—to love and to do good works.

Watching people arrive at church on Sunday morning is interesting. People are getting ready for a worship experience. They're getting ready to enter into the presence of God and to draw near to Him. When people gather for worship, each person has tremendous power and influence over the other people who are there. When someone walks into the house of God, a word spoken by a brother or sister in Christ has the power to lift them and encourage or to bring down and discourage.

When you come to church next Sunday morning, you'll have the opportunity to provoke the people you encounter. You can provoke them into hatred and doing wrong; you can provoke them into discouragement; you can provoke them into apathy, or you can provoke them unto love and to good works.

This verse reminds us that worship is about more than just me. I've heard some people say: "I can worship anywhere. I don't need to go to the Lord's house to worship." That's true. You can worship in lots of places. You can come into the presence of God in lots of places, but worship includes more than that. Worship includes considering one another and provoking one another in the direction of love and good works.

Worship is exercising our faithfulness.—Hebrews 10:25 says that we should not forsake the assembling of ourselves together. Worship is exercising our faithfulness. Let me remind you to whom the Book of Hebrews was written. In the beginning verses of the book, the author of Hebrews addresses this book to the Hebrew people who have been dispersed. The 12 tribes of Israel had been persecuted and forced to leave their homes. They had been dispersed throughout the known world. To this persecuted group, to these people who had lost their jobs and their homes because of their faith in Christ, the author said, "Don't forsake the assembling of yourselves together."

What a powerful statement! Here were people who could have lost their jobs or lost their way of providing an income for their families or lost their businesses or lost their homes because of attending a worship service. Yet in spite of the threat of severe persecution, the author of Hebrews admonished the Hebrew people not to forsake assembling themselves together.

I'm reminded of the women who went to Jesus' tomb early on that first Easter Sunday morning. Imagine what they had been through. They had seen the crucifixion and experienced the agonizing day of standing near the foot of the cross and seeing all the suffering Jesus endured. Along with that came a great deal of fear and concern and disruption of their daily lives. When that Sunday morning arrived, they must have been exhausted. They must have spent sleepless nights, and they must have been fearful at every sound they heard in the streets outside their homes. But in spite of their discouragement and fear, they got up and went to the tomb where Jesus had been laid.

Imagine what they would have missed if they had fallen for the devil's temptation to stay at home that day. They would have missed one of the greatest blessings in the history of Christianity. They were the ones who had the privilege of hearing the angels say, "He is not here; for he has risen" (Matt. 28:6).

I wonder if we ever miss opportunities because we forsake the assembling of ourselves together. Maybe we're tired, and maybe we're a little bit sick, or maybe we're just discouraged and downhearted on that day, and the devil tempts us just to stay home. Let's just wrap our blankets of pity and frustration and doubt around our shoulders, sit back in an easy chair, stay home, and take care of ourselves today. That's tempting sometimes, but what a blessing we might miss. What joy might escape us? What tremendous opportunity might present itself to us when the church assemblies for worship? The Lord instructs us that worship is exercising faithfulness because we as Christians need to take full advantage of every opportunity to worship Him. Worship is exercising our faithfulness.

Preparation for Worship

Worship is an encounter with God. Any time we come into His presence, worship takes place. When God's people gather for a worship service, we as leaders have the opportunity to lead them to worship, that is, lead them into the presence of God. Here are a few ideas to help you plan meaningful worship experiences.

Pray.—As a pastor, you would not think of preaching without spending much time in prayer. Just as preaching is important enough to deserve prayer time, so is all the worship time. Spend quality time seeking the will of God concerning each worship service. Whether you are a single-staff pastor, a leader of a volunteer, or a bivocational staff team, you as pastor should lead the way in prayer.

Plan well; be intentional.—I have an embarrassing confession to make. In my earliest years as a pastor, I would take last week's bulletin, white out the hymn numbers, type in some new ones, and call that worship planning. It was not. Intentional planning means developing the entire service around a theme. It means giving time and attention to all the details of the worship service.

Plan something fresh each week.—You've experienced moments in worship when something fresh happens and participants share a warm, genuine sense of the presence of God. Perhaps the fresh moment comes when a simple, sincere prayer touches hearts. It may come as a child reads Scripture or when a chorus is tagged unexpectedly to a familiar hymn.

If you announce the name and number of the chorus, it is not fresh. Just sing it. For example, tag the first verse of "Amazing Grace" to the end of "Nothing but the Blood." If you announce the name and number of "Amazing Grace," it is just another hymn. But if you just go into it, it is a fresh moment. If you pray about each service, God will give you one fresh moment for each service.

Enhance corporate prayer times.—Praying during a worship service is different from private prayer time. Prayer during a worship service is a conversation with God, but it is not a private conversation. The one who leads in public prayer speaks, in a sense, for the entire congregation. While you cannot provide a scripted prayer for those who lead in corporate prayer, you can attempt to improve corporate prayer in your services.

- Train deacons to lead in public prayer.
- Ask all worship leaders (including those who will lead in prayer) to gather for prayer before the worship service. In a sentence or two, interpret the focus of the worship time for that day. Encourage those who will lead in prayer to address the theme in their prayer.
- Use a Sunday or Wednesday night to teach your people about corporate prayer.

None of these ideas will completely solve the problem, but each of them will help.

Make giving time meaningful.—Giving is an act of worship. It is not just a time of collecting money.

- Train ushers to give every worshiper the opportunity to participate by holding the offering plate even if they have already given during Sunday School.
- Talk to your people about giving as an act of worship. Remind them of this just before the offering is given.
- Consider leading the congregation to read a worship passage aloud together just before the offering. Print the passage in the bulletin.

Eliminate dead time.—Ask all those who will speak or lead to come to the platform before their appointed time and be ready to begin without delay when their time comes. Those who sing a solo or in small groups can usually make their way to the platform during the hymn that precedes their presentation. By the way, most introductions are unnecessary if you use a bulletin or worship guide.

Strive for excellence.—This Sunday your congregation will gather at the house of God. They will come with all kinds of needs. The one thing they will all have in common is a need to encounter God. Let no poorly planned moment stand in the way. Regardless of the worship style you find comfortable, strive for excellence in everything you do.

Worship Planning in a Team

Plan with the song leader to make worship meaningful.[1]

Plan the services together.—No one person has all the answers as to what a worship service should be. Put your best thinking and ideas on the worship-planning table. Let them mingle with ideas from other people. Remember, the worship service is not to be a showcase for the creativity of a human leader but rather a time when God is allowed to speak and manifest Himself in any number of ways.

If you cannot sit down and plan with your song leader, at least tell him the subject of your sermon.—This comment is almost always in first place on the list of expectations music leaders have of their pastors. While nearly all church music leaders can recount numerous times when they had to plan blindly for a service with no clue as to the sermon topic or theme, they've also marveled at how the Holy Spirit has merged the efforts of the pastor and music director into one spiritually moving and unified service. "If God can bless our efforts with little or no planning, how much more could He bless us with even a little planning for our shared worship experience?" more than one music director has asked.

Your song leader needs more lead time to prepare for Sunday services.—Music leaders have numerous persons to get ready for their involvement in the worship service including the choir, soloists, instrumentalists, sound and light technicians, dramatists, and ensembles. Give your music leaders as much lead time as you possibly can.

Help your song leader access some training opportunities.—Few volunteer music leaders can afford to take time away from their vocations and spend their own limited funds to secure training. But with encouragement from the pastor and funds for expenses from the church, most volunteer leaders will agree to take some training.

Whether the music leader in a church is paid or unpaid, everyone likes to be appreciated.—Pastor, commend your song leader when he does a good job; redirect him when he doesn't. An occasional good word, pat on the back, and public recognition provide affirmation. The pastor's leadership in these areas is important.

Help your song leader to identify traditional church music practices and customs and not to make hasty decisions regarding change.—It's sometimes difficult for a minister of music, new to a church, to recognize traditional church music practices and customs within a congregation.

Your song leader can be your best minister of music if he knows and understands your goals and desires for the church as a whole and your work habits and preferences.—Many times he is kept in the dark about your preferences and sense of direction. Share confidentially with him. Pray and share spiritual moments together. He is a member of your team, and his desire is to support you in every way possible as the spiritual leader of the church. Help him to do that.

Ideas to Involve Children in Worship

Too often, children are expected to experience genuine worship even though the worship service is designed completely for adults.[2] You and I are much more likely to worship when we are participants in worship, not just observers. The same is true for children. Here are a few ways to involve children in worship.

Schedule an "Invitation to Worship" meeting involving parents and children.—Promote the meeting in children's and parent's Sunday School classes, the church newsletter and bulletin, and other ministries that touch children or their parents. Use the meeting to accomplish three things.

1. Discuss ways to help children experience God in worship. Use the ideas uncovered during this meeting throughout the year.

2. Educate parents about the importance of worship for their children. Enlist their support and help in involving children in worship.

3. Encourage family worship times.

Ask children to read Scripture during a worship service.—Choose children who are ready to do this. Avoid situations that might embarrass a child.

Ask children to lead the congregation in prayer.—Ask the child well in advance. Help parents prepare the child for this responsibility.

Enlist and train children to receive the offering from time to time.— You may choose to enlist adults to participate alongside children.

Preach a children's sermon.—This may be a regular feature in which you share a lesson designed especially for children. It may also be a way to present the sermon with a special focus for children.[3]

Calendar a Sunday as "Children's Day."—Recognize children in the morning worship service, and invite children and families to a church-sponsored picnic that afternoon. Be sure you, as pastor, attend and participate. The children need to get to know you in an informal setting.

Consider using a printed listening sheet for children to use during worship.—You may choose to give children a small reward if they show you the completed listening sheet following the service. Here are some sample questions for the listening sheet.

My name is _____.

I am sitting in church with _____.

The song we sang in church that I liked best was_____.

The special music this morning was _____.

The Scripture reading this morning was from:

book_____ chapter _____ verse _____.

The name of a person who led in prayer was _____.

Here is one thing the pastor said _____.

Ask the adult choir or an adult who sings a special to sing a children's song and dedicate it to the children in the worship service.

Invite the children's choir to sing during the worship service.

Ask a child to play a musical instrument as part of a praise time.

Involve missions education organizations by asking children to provide a missions moment during the worship service.—This feature should present or interpret some missionary person or ministry.

Invite a child to give a personal testimony entitled "I'm Glad I'm a Christian because. . . ."

Ways Drama Can Enhance Worship Times

Meaningful, relevant drama requires planning. Here are some easy ways to make dramatic changes in your smaller membership church.

Instead of simply having one person read the Scripture, have two or three people divide the Scriptures into parts and read it.—For instance, read the story of Adam and Eve, using a narrator, someone reading Adam's words, another reading Eve's, another reading the serpent's, and one reading God's lines.

Have someone learn the American Sign Language interpretation of a familiar hymn, and let someone sign the words as the congregation sings.—Someone in your congregation may already know sign language and would love to help you with this.

Allow your youth to act out one of their favorite Christian songs.— They will enjoy doing this, and you'll be surprised by their insight and creativity. Be sure to give them some adult supervision.

Buy a subscription to National Drama Service (available on the Dated Order Forms or by calling 1-800-458-2772).—This quarterly publication of scripts gives you photocopy rights to all the material. Most require limited props and lighting. Scripts are short enough to be incorporated into a traditional worship gathering.

Preach through the beatitudes and have teams of youth or adults assigned to improvise a situation that illustrates a certain beatitude.— Give each team a few weeks' notice. If you keep encouraging them, you'll be surprised what they might create! (This would work with many other series, such as the phrases of the Lord's prayer, the parables, and others.)

Use sound effects during Scripture readings.—Sound effects tapes are easily found in most music stores. Imagine reading the parable of the wise and foolish builders with the sounds of construction and then sounds of a coming storm!

Candles can add drama to any service.—Try turning off the lights, lighting a candle, and reading the following monologue:

This Little Light of Mine

We loved the light, so we built a church around it to shelter if from the cold, dark world.

And every Monday night we take it out to visit those who saw the light last Sunday.

We have matchbooks we carry with us, but we're afraid to use them for fear that something might catch fire and we wouldn't be able to control it.

So we leave the candle at the church where we can visit it whenever we want.

We love our light, but it seems these days that the light is getting dim—perhaps because it's running out of oxygen due to the walls we've built around it.

Every now and then I wonder what would happen if we opened the door and let the fire warm and the light shine, but we've grown quite accustomed to the darkness.

Hide it under a bushel? No!

We'd much prefer hiding it in a church.

We know Satan would never find it there; would he?

(Pause, next line to be sung)

Don't let Satan—

(Blow out the candle).[4]

Use reader's theater.—It's easy and nonthreatening to the untrained dramatist. It requires rehearsal, familiarity, and expression; but it doesn't require memorization.

Read the famous poem "Touch of the Master's Hand."—Hold a violin as you read about the auction, then have a violinist come out of the audience and play it as you read the concluding verses of the poem.

Encourage your artistic members to express their gift in the life of your church.—For some it will be storytelling, painting, song writing, acting, or clowning. For others it may be suggesting a concept that someone else may be able to interpret. If you open the door for drama, done with excellence and creativity, it will breathe new vitality and vision to whatever church you are serving.[5]

---

[1] The following section was adapted from the writings of Danny Jones, manager, Field Services Section, Music Ministries Department, LifeWay Christian Resources of the Southern Baptist Convention.

[2] The following section was adapted from Rosey Davis, "Involving Children in Worship," *Church Administration*, December 1989, 22-23.

[3] For ongoing help with children's sermons and additional ideas for involving children in worship, see *Let's Worship*, a quarterly publication for comprehensive worship planning. Available from LifeWay Christian Resources of the Southern Baptist Convention. For more information, call 1-800-458-2772.

[4] For a wealth of readers material, get Matt Tullos, compiler, *The Imaginary Stage* from LifeWay Christian Resources. Call 1-800-458-2772. This is a book of easy-to-do reader's theater sketches.

[5] This section is based on the writings of Matt Tullos, a Vacation Bible School editor in the Sunday School Division, LifeWay Christian Resources.

Are YOU living in a FISHBOWL

The *Minister's Family* can help!

No magazine can take you out of the fishbowl, but *Minister's Family* will enable you and your family to manage life in the fishbowl "swimmingly."

The new *Minister's Family* magazine addresses the <u>tough</u> personal issues you face each and every day:

- Handling the stresses of church and home
- Coping with loneliness and isolation
- Raising children in full view of the church
- Improving relations with your spouse
- Increasing your savings and planning for retirement
- Plus <u>more</u> issues unique to the ministry

Minister's Family helps meet *your* needs so you can better meet the needs of others! Whether you're a pastor, bivocational minister, minister of education, minister of music, age group staff minister, chaplain, missionary, or in <u>any</u> other ministry position, *Minister's Family* is for you.

Minister's Family is just $18.28* a year for all four refreshing and encouraging issues. *Email* your subscription request to *customerservice@lifeway.com* or *fax* <u>anytime</u> to *(615) 251-5933*. If you prefer, order *Minister's Family* with your current LifeWay Quarterly Order Packet under the *Church Staff Periodicals* heading on the DATED RESOURCES FORM.

Just read one issue of *Minister's Family* and you'll be "hooked."